The Death Drive

Why Societies Self-Destruct

D1566104

Niklas Hageback

The Death Drive

Why Societies Self-Destruct

GAUDIUM

Gaudium Publishing

Las Vegas ◊ Oxford ◊ Palm Beach

Published in the United States of America by
Histria Books, a division of Histria LLC
7181 N. Hualapai Way
Las Vegas, NV 89166 USA
HistriaBooks.com

Gaudium Publishing is an imprint of Histria Books. Titles published under the imprints of Histria Books are exclusively distributed worldwide through the Casemate Group.

Library of Congress Control Number: 2019951301

ISBN 978-1-59211-032-2 (hardcover)
ISBN 978-1-59211-034-6 (softbound)

Table of Contents

Introduction

Tolerance and apathy are the last two virtues of a dying society

— Aristotle, Greek philosopher (384-322 B.C.)

The notion that instincts influence behavior has long been disdained by political science, mankind is considered to be ruled by rationality alone, hence political and economic systems are designed to be optimized for rationality. In biology and clinical psychology though, human instincts are an undisputed and uncontroversial fact, albeit generally labelled drives or innate tendencies. However, these psychological forces are nevertheless overlooked as root causes of societal actions, why is that? Is it because they are an ugly reminder of an uncivilized past we want to be as far as possibly detached from? But if a society operates on assumed rationality alone, implicitly rejecting certain instinctual manifestations, will its ability to govern be hampered and it is doomed to experience collective bursts of violence and destruction? A review of political history does paint a picture of a troublesome recurring irrational dysfunctionality that has proven hard to explain and forecast.

Psychology shows that the repressions of instincts do have reper-
cussions, and dire ones at that, something which has been thoroughly
examined at both the individual and collective levels, and its symptoms
well are recognized: anxiety, neurosis and other psychological ailments.
And if these are allowed to linger on, they eventually erupt in destructive behavior, either directed inwards or targeting external objects. In
other words, can a society self-destruct due to psychological forces?

But why would individuals and collectives follow a self-destructive
path which, on a superficial level, appears to be in stark contradiction
with the survival instinct? A number of psychological theories have
evolved to explain this conundrum, starting with Sigmund Freud and
what he referred to as the *death drive* (Der Todestrieb). The death drive
can be described as a basic psychological mechanism that reflects the
repressed instincts' pursuit to undermine the reigning moral, political,
or cultural narratives in order to set them free. Whilst this more than a
century-old theory might seem antiquated, recent findings in neuroscience, most notably *neuro-psychoanalytics*, breathe new life in it by con-
firming the existence of an unconscious that plays an active part in decision-making and how perceptions are interpreted. Freud viewed the
unconscious as a dustbin of sorts which stored repressed emotions and
desires, deemed 'forbidden' by societal norms and, although repressed,
they kept impacting behavior with a predilection to trigger neurosis, including aggression, directed either inwards or outwards. So, with recent
findings in neuroscience supporting key elements of Freud's theories,
maybe he was onto something after all.

However, the death drive remains among the most controversial
concepts in psychoanalysis, something which post-Freudians never

could reach consensus on, and over time it fell in oblivion. Hence, contemporary writings remain scarce.

But witnessing the political upheavals and turmoil of recent years, in what was supposed to be mankind's *nirvana*, namely the liberal democracy and the global market economy, they have shown that the reigning academic political science and conflict theories are not standing up to reality. Societal breakdowns, with apparently self-destructive characteristics, appear when theoretically they should not exist, permeating and superseding acts of *supposed* rationality. Thus, the question now merits to be posed; *are these manifestations of the death drive?*

Attempts to forecast societal breakdowns, including revolutions and wars, have been numerous over the centuries, even millennia; from the fall of the Roman Empire, the French Revolution, the Russian Revolution and, more recently, the fall of Communism in Eastern Europe and the Arab Spring, whose outcomes, in parts, are still unfolding. However, these events all share a single commonality; they took their contemporary world by surprise. In hindsight, of course, the developments seemed anything but surprising and historians elaborate on lengthy explanations about the *whys* and the *whens*. But without the apparent retrospective view at hand, these events do appear as lightning striking from a clear sky. Clearly, something has been missing in the existing methodologies and with the current turbulence in both the European and American political systems, many concerned voices have been raised asking whether we are yet again entering an era of conflict.

The key question therefore remains unanswered; *why did these events that undermined the existing political arrangements take place at the time they did?* Existing conflict theories generally manage to unmask the structural factors considered explanatory root causes, whether they are of a social, economic, or political nature. But typically, these factors can have been in place for decades, sometimes even centuries. Where the standard models consistently fail are in defining and highlighting the triggers that ignite abrupt change and what heralds it. Anecdotally, certain (self-)destructive sentiments seem to suddenly hold sway whereby the established order, *the status quo*, simply must be destroyed and the psychological urges to do so have become too great to resist. Any student of Freudian psychoanalysis will immediately recognize this phenomena as the death drive at work, seeking to break down a societal and civil order that has become too repressive for the mental well-being of its denizens in an environment where anxiety and neurosis have become commonplace.

If we accept a psychological force with death drive characteristics playing a role in the human makeup, would such phenomena help to explain the recurring irrational behavior that seems to haunt our modern societies and which may now be unfolding throughout large parts of the world? By venturing to develop a model that captures the settings that prompt and exacerbate the ignition of the death drive, the prediction of societal destructive behavior, manifested in one way or another, becomes feasible. This path has, however, often been shunned by mainstream academics and for good reasons; the accuracy in measuring something as elusive, yet palpable, as a collective psychological state of mind has, to date, not rendered any robust results, other than providing eyewitness accounts that provide color to historical events. Often interesting, but rarely convincing and conclusive. Thus, the lack of a verifiable method has proven to be an insurmountable stumbling block.

Attempting to develop a death drive measurement methodology means applying meta-level philosophical ponderings on what is *normal,* and how to define normal behavior, as the death drive is best examined against a fluctuating normality. As Freud posited, instincts and civilization need not always be conflicting, it is the psychologically healthy society's aspiration to align and direct instincts towards outlets within its confinements of acceptable norms and morals. But if not successful, repression will dawn and the first signs are mental rigidity and sterility, which causes stagnation and apathy, typically projected into banal or secular matters, and if not appropriately addressed in a timely manner, risks trigger bizarre manifestations which are the precursors to social unrest of varying degree.

One reasonable starting point in defining and determining the settings that are susceptible to these tendencies is to work backwards from historical outbreaks of social upheavals, whether in the form of revolutions, regime breakdowns, or outright wars. Based on these historical cases, one can attempt to draw out and crafts metrics to distinguish values that only appear in psychologically 'damaged' societies, thereby providing a delineation to ascertain trigger points in terms of themes, duration, and frequency.

In the pages that follow, I will offer an explanatory framework and measurement methodology to predict periods of destruction that often have grim effects on societies. In doing so, I will reveal the limitations of the methods of modern political science and its inadequate policy-making in defining and managing the psychological workings of mankind. The result will be a model to better understand and forecast the seemingly irrational destructive human forces that hold such great and sinister influence on world affairs.

PSYCHOANANLYSIS – A PRIMER

This chapter provides the layman reader with a limited understanding of psychoanalysis with the definitions and insights to the various concepts that are being discussed in the succeeding chapter, this to empower and facilitate the reading. Anyone already familiar with psychoanalysis can omit this chapter, as some later sections are partly overlapping.

Despite the human fascination for psychology, which can trace its roots to the earliest days of mankind, a number of key concepts such as *the mind, the unconscious,* and *free will* are still hard to pin down and exactly define, which to some extent has held back scientific progress in the understanding of the human mental apparatus.

The Mind

The function of the human mind, and especially how it relates to the body, has been deliberated going back millennia, and the debate is yet to be concluded. Strange as it might seem, something so essential in defining the human species still remains elusive and difficult to grasp. The concept of the human mind has been studied from many perspectives; historically, as part of religion and philosophy, and in modern times directed toward psychology and, more recently, neuroscience. What has and has not been considered as part of the faculties of the mind has differed over time, however a current definition of the mind reads:

> *the collective conscious and unconscious processes in a sentient organism that direct and influence mental and physical behavior.*[1]

The elements of sentience being the brain, nerve processes, cognition, and the motor and sensory processes.

But its exact traits remain the subject of academic debate and have yet to be precisely defined. Some argue that only "higher" intellectual functions constitute the mind, in particular reason, imagination, and memory, while emotions such as love, hate, fear, and joy are of a more instinctual character and should be excluded. Others hold that rational and emotional (read: irrational) states cannot be so distinctly separated as their origins are shared, so both are considered to be part of the mind. What is generally acknowledged is that the mind includes attributes such as perceptions, reason, imagination, awareness, memories, emotions, and a faculty for exchanging information.

The current focus of research which is geared towards neuroscience and the *man-machine* relationship is putting the biological perspective in the forefront. It has been evidenced that certain functions of the mind

---

[1]*The American Heritage Dictionary of the English Language.* http://ahdictionary.com/ (accessed January 1, 2019).

can be pinned to certain parts of the brain. The study of patients with brain damage shows that injuries to specific parts of the brain result in impairments in functions seen as part of the mind. Experiments with drugs have also revealed brain-mind links, for example, sedatives reduce awareness while stimulants do the opposite. But the advances of neuroscience and genetics have not yet provided a comprehensive picture of how the brain produces and relates to various functions of the mind. For example, although some emotions can be directly related to certain brain structures, neuroscience still falls far short in fully explaining emotions in terms of brain processes.[2] An important concept in the debate is *qualia*, the individual subjective description of a perception or experience, such as describing an emotion, the level of pain, describing a color, how something tastes or smells, and so on. In essence, *qualia* means that it is difficult to objectively describe an experience without it containing a subjective element that others can find difficult to understand or relate to. *Qualia* brings the mind-body problem to its core as so far it has not been possible to neuro-scientifically explain the subjective 'making sense' of a certain experience and why it can differ from person to person.[3]

---

[2]Computational Neuroscience Research Group. Waterloo Centre for Theoretical Neuroscience. http://compneuro.uwaterloo.ca/ index.html (accessed January 1, 2019).

[3]Kriegel, Uriah. *Current Controversies in Philosophy of Mind* (New York, NY: Taylor & Francis, 2014) p. 201.

Instincts

The concept of instincts has evolved since it was introduced into the field of psychology by the German psychologist Wilhelm Wundt (1832-1920) in the 1870s. Initially, most repetitive behavior was considered instinctual, over time, however, in the 1960s, the American psychologist Abraham Maslow (1908-1970) argued that humans do not have instincts, as evidenced by the fact that we are able to override them. Citing the reproductive instinct and the survival instinct, Maslow pointed out that some women deliberately choose not to have children, that some mothers suffering depression have been known to kill their own children, and that some people choose to commit suicide. Maslow felt that although the overriding of the reproductive and survival instincts often coincided with mental illnesses, human ability to deliberately interfere with them diluted the concept of humans having instincts, unlike animals. He and his contemporaries saw instincts rather as strong biological tendencies and motivators for certain human behaviors, but they distinguished them from (animal) instincts and referred to them as *drives*.[4]

The most up-to-date research supports the existence of drives, or *innate abilities* as they are now commonly referred to. Regardless of how they are labelled, they have a strong tendency to influence behavior whether that be on an individual level or in groups bounded by genetic clusters, thus their influence is estimated on a probabilistic scale rather than a deterministic one. So, the current view is that humans have *drives*,

---

[4]Maslow, Abraham H. "Instinct Theory Reexamined" in *Motivation and Personality* (New York: Harper & Row, 1954).

which unlike instincts can be deliberately overridden, but generally they are not. These drives usually involve a greater degree of 'education' than that of animal instincts, and they can be situation-dependently flexible. The academic discipline that studies human behavior from a biological perspective, *socio-biology*, does not consider there to be defined human instincts, but rather *biological bases* for human behavior – possibly just more word play to avoid the use of the term "instinct."[5]

Reflexes, on the other hand, are a simpler form of behavioral pattern. The stimulus in a reflex may not even require brain activity, like the message flowing to the spinal cord and then being transmitted back without travelling to the brain through a path called the reflex arc[6] – for example, the involuntary kick your doctor generates when he taps your knee with a hammer.

Free Will

The question whether humans have *free will* is closely linked with the notion of awareness. Free will is defined as:

---

[5]Mandal, Fatik Baran. *Textbook of Animal Behaviour* (Delhi: PHI Learning, 2010).

[6]*Merck Manual of Diagnosis and Therapy Home Edition*, "Physical Examination," 06-077c, www.merckmanuals.com (accessed January 1, 2019).

"the ability to make choices free from certain kinds of constraints; constraints might be of a physical, biological, social/cultural, or psychological nature."[7]

There are two broad schools of thought arguing over the existence of free will. *Determinism* contests free will, with the basic assumption that present actions are caused by the past; in other words, every decision one makes is driven by preceding events, which, in turn, are driven by the events preceding them, in a causal chain that prevents one from acting independently and exercising choice. The other school of thought is *libertarianism*, which assumes humans to be rational agents with a capacity to make free choices among alternatives.[8]

Between these opposing views are a number of variations and combinations that relax some of the more definite conditions; for example, even if causality exists, humans still have the option to choose their actions, such as at any time making the voluntary decision to end one's own life. Other variations propose predestined outcomes or goals, but state that the paths to arrive there come with free choice.

The free will debate has implications that impact religious, ethical, judicial, and scientific thought. If free will can be demonstrated not to exist, can a person then be held legally and morally accountable for his actions, if these are predetermined and cannot be influenced? From a scientific viewpoint, if actions are anchored in past events, is it possible

---

[7]"Free Will," in *The Stanford Encyclopedia of Philosophy*, ed. Edward N. Zalta (Summer 2011 Edition), http://plato.stanford.edu/ (accessed January 1, 2019).

[8]*The American Heritage Dictionary of the English Language.* http://ahdictionary .com/ (accessed January 1, 2019).

to make forecasts and produce statistical probabilities on predictable outcomes? It also involves the concept of drives; if in a certain situation strong biological motivators are triggered, albeit possible to override but highly unlikely so, do we then have free will? As with so many of the key concepts in psychology, the study of free will remains open and has moved from the academic areas of religion and philosophy to neuroscience and medicine. The definition of a *death drive* builds on the assumption that free will has psychological limitations, underpinning biological forces, by which mankind is constrained.

The Unconscious

Although there is broad acceptance among psychologists and neuroscientists of the existence of an unconscious part of the mind and its ability to affect thoughts and behavior, its exact functions and processes have yet to be determined.

It is important to distinguish between unconsciousness and the unconscious. Unconsciousness is a mental state during which there is little or no response to external stimuli, such as being asleep or in a coma. The unconscious, however, is defined as:

"processes in the mind that occur automatically and are not available to introspection, and include thought processes, memory, affect, and motivation."[9]

---

[9]*Merriam-Webster Dictionary*, www.merriam-webster.com/ (accessed January 1, 2019).

Initially, the unconscious was equated with unintentional acts as it coincided with the development of hypnosis in the mid-1800s and its enthusiastic exploitation in vaudeville stage performances. The strange and often bizarre acts of volunteers after being induced into a hypnotic state – a state in which behavior, as it was claimed, could be dictated, but about which the subject had no memory – popularized the idea that there is a part of the mind about which we are unaware but that can be addressed, and can influence our behavior, seemingly against our conscious will.[10] How could a hypnotist make suggestions to subjects who are apparently asleep – though a strange form of sleep in which they can open their eyes and follow instructions – if not for the existence of an unconscious with the power to control actions?

With the theories presented by Sigmund Freud and Carl Gustav Jung in the early twentieth century, the understanding of the unconscious would be much improved and a lot of their findings still stand today.

Sigmund Freud

The Austrian psychologist Sigmund Freud (1856-1939) greatly advanced the fledgling discipline of psychology, particularly in developing the theories of the unconscious. His early work focused on neurotic symptoms and traumatic memories. Through his interaction with patients, he arrived at the belief that an important factor in the development of neurosis, such as acting in ways not conforming to the reigning

---

[10]Ellenberger, Henri F. *The Discovery of the Unconscious: The History and Evolution of Dynamic Psychiatry* (New York: Basic Books, 1970).

socially acceptable norms, was due to the repression of forbidden emotions or desires. Freud regarded the unconscious as a hidden cupboard of sorts where these forbidden thoughts were shut away as they could not be erased from memory. In particular, he felt that the repression of sexual thoughts and fantasies from early childhood into the unconscious was a key factor in a person developing neurosis. Freud explored techniques to draw out repressed memories from the unconscious, including hypnosis and dream analysis, and eventually he developed his own method, with patients lying on a couch and encouraged to speak their minds freely. By analyzing the symbolic meaning of their relaxed ramblings, he found hints as to the nature of their emotional states and neurosis. Freud referred to this technique as *psychoanalysis*, and it was to become his landmark contribution to psychology. Its aim was to draw repressed thoughts and desires back into the conscious because, according to him, it is then that patients can acknowledge and release the repressed emotions and thereby eventually free themselves from neurosis.[11]

Freud summed up the features of the unconscious in his 1915 essay, *The Unconscious*:

> *It can be contradictory; opposing feelings or wishes can coexist. For example, you can feel love and hate for the same thing at the same time;*
>
> *Repressed thoughts or emotions are likely to return to the conscious in some form;*

---

[11]Sheehy, Noel & Forsythe, Alexandra. "Sigmund Freud," in *Fifty Key Thinkers in Psychology* (London: Routledge, 2013).

The unconscious is timeless; its contents have no chronological order, the cause and effect relationship can be put out of play, and;

In people with a mental disorder, it can thrust itself into the conscious and replace physical reality with psychic reality, such as fantasies, dreams and symbolism.[12]

As Freud gained more insight into the workings of the mind, he concluded that it was fueled by flows of psychic energy, which he labelled *libido.* As with any energy in a closed system, the level of libido in the mind is constant, hence an examination of the direction and intensity of its flow will give the psychoanalyst indications to imbalances between the conscious and the unconscious.

Initially, Freud considered the libido to be connected with mankind's sexual development and desires, but later he came to see it as flowing back and forth between the conscious and the unconscious under the influence of two innate forces. The first he called *the pleasure principle*, which triggers the impulse to seek immediate gratification of wishes and urges, not exclusively sexual ones. Freud saw the pleasure principle as the main drive of unconscious desires. The other force he called *the reality principle.* It resides in the conscious and reins in the impulses seeking immediate gratification.[13]

To fend off the drives and urges from the unconscious, as to conform with societal norms, the mind deploys *defense mechanisms*, usually

---

[12]Freud, Sigmund. *The Unconscious* (London: Penguin Modern Classics Translated Texts, 2005).

[13]Freud, Sigmund. *Group Psychology and the Analysis of the Ego* (New York: Bantam Books, 1960).

at the unconscious level, to subdue these. There are a number of defense mechanisms and some with overlapping features, sometimes making them hard to precisely distinguish, but the following are the most important ones;[14]

Repression: an impulse that forces something emotionally painful to be forgotten and consigned to the unconscious. Because the psychological issue has not been dealt with or resolved by the conscious, it continues to affect the person unconsciously and can eventually develop into mental disorders. For example, a person who represses memories of abuse experienced during childhood is likely to have difficulties forming relationships until the repressed feelings have been addressed.

Suppression: a conscious act to forget something, in an attempt to cope with a troubling situation. Suppression is similar to repression, but the unpleasant feelings are pushed down consciously rather than unconsciously, and to the preconscious rather than the unconscious, and are therefore easier to bring back and address at a later stage. For example, a person may temporarily suppress violent impulses stemming from being delayed by a traffic jam and release them later in socially acceptable behavior, such as through aggressive sports.

Projection: a person or group unconsciously projects thoughts or feelings not tolerated by the ego onto others, thereby creating scapegoats for particular issues. One of the most notorious collective examples is the Nazis' blaming the Jewish population for Germany's defeat in World War I.

---

[14]Freud, Anna. *The Ego and the Mechanisms of Defense* (London: Karnac Books, 1992).

Condensation: in which several concepts, usually including aggressive or sexual impulses, are blended with other nonthreatening concepts and suppressed into the unconscious. This produces a single symbol to represent the combined components. This symbol becomes a figurative form to represent the suppressed impulses.

Denial: a person or group denies reality by pretending it does not exist, like the deluded ruler and his subjects in the tale of the "*Emperor's New Clothes.*" Examples include someone told he has a terminal illness who will initially go through a stage of denial, pretending this is not the case, before reality finally sinks in.

Displacement: the redirecting of feelings or actions from a dangerous outlet to a safer one; for example, a person yelling at his secretary after being reprimanded by his boss.

Rationalization: to seek a rational explanation or justification for upsetting actions or behavior caused by factors too unpleasant to acknowledge; for example, a person whose application for a job is rejected and who rationalizes the failure by claiming he was not really that interested in the job. Another example is a student who fails a test and rationalizes that it was the result of poor teaching and not his lack of preparation. Rationalization protects the ego by avoiding or circumventing the true reason for events or behaviors, whether or not controllable.

Reaction formation: the disguising of beliefs or impulses, considered unacceptable, by the exaggerated expression of opposite beliefs or impulses. For example, some men unhappily possess homosexual tendencies and suppress these tendencies; they then project instead a hatred of homosexuals; they attack in others what they hate in themselves.

Regression: the return to a previous stage of mental development in a situation of adversity, such as an adult acting childishly in response to an unfavorable situation, say, by refusing to leave bed, or hiding under the blankets in bed, after a bad day at work.

Sublimation: the acting out of unacceptable impulses in a socially acceptable way, such as by finding outlets for the libido in athletic, cultural or intellectual pursuits.

Carl Gustav Jung

Carl Gustav Jung (1875-1961) was a Swiss psychologist and for a time one of Freud's closest disciples. At first, he subscribed to Freud's theories, but eventually he started to diverge, among others, he saw Freud's view of the unconscious as incomplete. Whereas Freud viewed it as a dustbin for repressed emotions and desires rejected by the conscious, Jung believed it played a more active role in the mind. He also dismissed Freud's models of the mind as arbitrary and too simplistic.[15] Jung, who based his empirical work on patients and wider historical research, started to develop his own theory and, while he shared Freud's view that the mind is divided into two parts, the conscious and the unconscious, which interact with each other, he saw additional dimensions of the mind: the personal and the collective. Whereas the personal conscious is unique to each individual, the collective conscious is

[15]Dunne, Claire. *Carl Jung: Wounded Healer of the Soul: An Illustrated Biography* (London: Continuum International Publishing Group, 2002).

a form of public opinion, a distillation of what has become the average person's cultural and moral values into a set of societal beliefs, norms, attitudes, and mainstream political *-isms*. The values held in the collective conscious tend to be shared among the greater majority of individuals of the group and with the shared values generally superseding and repressing any conflicting personal beliefs or values.

The personal unconscious is defined by Jung as containing:

> *lost memories, painful ideas that are repressed (i.e. forgotten on purpose), subliminal perceptions, by which are meant sense-perceptions that were not strong enough to reach consciousness, and finally, contents that are not yet ripe for consciousness.*[16]

Hence, the contents of the personal unconscious are unique to each individual much like that of the personal conscious. Jung's definition of the personal unconscious comes close to Freud's view of the unconscious; however, he came to believe that something in Freud's model was missing, questioning the assumption that the human mind develops from a blank slate, *tabula rasa*, at birth. He hypothesized that innate, universal patterns existed in the unconscious – separate from the personal unconscious – and that these patterns could influence thought and behavior. Studying his patients' and his own dreams and reviewing diverse myths and sagas, these became the main conduits of exploring the unconscious. Jung identified recurring patterns of themes that seemed

---

[16]Jung, C. G. "The archetypes and the collective unconscious." In Part 1: *The Collected Works of C. G. Jung*, translated by RFC Hull (Princeton, NJ: Princeton University Press, Vol. 9, 2nd edition, 1981) par. 103.

to exist collectively regardless of era, culture, or geography – the arche-types (from the ancient Greek *arkhetupon*, which can be translated as an original model that can be copied). The universal patterns it contains are a form of genetic memory, the common experiences shared by human-ity that have become hard-coded into our DNA over millennia, forming a collective unconscious. Jung saw them as being part of man since the earliest days, shaped by evolution and representing the collective his-tory of the human species as the product of constantly repeated experi-ences.[17] These archetypes generally lie dormant in the collective uncon-scious, in other words they are not actively influencing thoughts and behaviors. But when a catalyst – an event or emotion in conscious reality – creates a sufficiently-strong psychological impetus, an archetype somehow related to that catalyst awakes and begins to stimulate the conscious and alter perceptions. Archetypal images begin to appear, usually as symbols in visions, dreams, language and other forms of ex-pressions, and eventually affect conscious thinking and prompt a psy-chological context in which differing sets of actions are likely to be taken compared to the pre-archetype era in order to rectify the psychological unbalances and reduce the likelihood for mental ill-health. Whereas in-stincts (*drives*) are triggers for specific behavior - for example, a percep-tion of danger activates the survival instinct, which then triggers the fight or flight response, archetypes regulate perceptions and thought patterns that create *tendencies* toward altering behavior, however with the shared aspiration of ensuring human survival, albeit with a longer-term focus. As archetypes reside in the collective unconscious, we are

---

[17]Stevens, Anthony & Rosen, David H. *The Two Million-Year-Old Self, Carolyn and Ernest Fay Series in Analytical Psychology* (College Station, TX: Texas A&M University Press, 2005).

neither aware of their existence nor of their influence on our perceptions. As such they are an invisible force, like that of a magnet attracting
items in its direction. Even as they become activated, affecting the behavior and how we grasp reality, they remain obscure as they have become such forming parts of our everyday discourse that we fail to notice
them. But eventually they are detectable through observing the foot-
prints they leave – these archetypal images emerge into our awareness
and over time become the narratives which inform our world views. It
is through the appearance of archetypal images in the conscious that we
are able to infer the existence of the archetypes themselves. In Jung's
own words:

> *Archetypes are irrepresentable in themselves but their effects are dis-*
> *cernible in archetypal images and motifs. Archetypes... present*
> *themselves as ideas and images, like everything else that becomes a*
> *content of consciousness.*[18]

Current Thinking

A century later, how do the theories of Freud and Jung stand up to
current thinking and the findings of neuroscience? And is there any evidence that supports the notion of conscious and unconscious parts of
the mind that forms holistic human thinking?

---

[18]Jung, C. G. "Concerning the archetypes and the anima concept." In Part 1: *The
Collected Works of C. G. Jung*, translated by RFC Hull. Princeton (NJ): Princeton
University Press, Vol. 9, 2nd edition, 1981), par. 136.

Psychology of today has expanded on Freud's notion of the unconscious. Each of psychology's multifaceted disciplines has its own doctrine and focus of research regarding the unconscious. In cognitive psychology, researchers are studying *implicit memory* – a type of memory in which previous experiences aid in the performing of a task without conscious awareness of these previous experiences. Psychologists have been investigating *priming* and *automaticity*, the ability to do something without being actively aware of it, such as repetitive menial tasks (for example, riding a bicycle). Another area of research involves the *unconscious acquisition of information*. While a person is not consciously aware of himself absorbing information, these processes can still influence behavior and decision-making processes. Empirical tests have shown that a person can act on information that was processed only in the unconscious *before* any awareness of that information or decision to act enters the conscious; for example, unconsciously determining patterns of sequences for various events. In tests, such as detecting the frequency of certain cards recurring in a deck of cards being displayed, subjects asked to pay specific attention to particular types of events and estimate their frequency are rarely able to provide better estimates than subjects given no hint beforehand of what they are to be asked to do.[19]

The scientific community now believes that the unconscious plays an active part in certain decision-making processes, which is a marked shift from Freud's image of the unconscious as a dustbin of repressed material. And the most current theories on the processes of the unconscious have a distinct advantage over Freud's anecdotal case studies;

---

[19]Dijksterhuis, Ap. et al. "The Unconscious Mind" *Perspectives on Psychological Science* 3, no. 1 (2008), pp. 73-79.

they are more data driven, and they lend themselves to clinical testing and empirical validation.

If certain decision-making processes take place outside the conscious, and some seem even not consciously intended, how they are accomplished remains an open question. Psychologists are also interested in how personal judgment and social behavior operate outside awareness and conscious intent. Similar questions have been addressed on research projects conducted in the areas of evolutionary biology and neuroscience. Currently there is agreement among the various sciences that a distinction can be made between unconscious processes and the unconscious mind. Cognitive research shows the unconscious to be part of an automatic process that registers and stores more information than experienced through the conscious. This appears to happen unintentionally, regardless of conscious goals and instructions. It seems to be a fully automatic process that is innate in all humans whatever their age, intelligence, culture, education, or other personal factors.[20]

While the unconscious acts as an independent agent outside the control of awareness, it also serves as a complementary partner to the conscious, manifesting itself usually in the form of intuition, gut feelings, *eureka* moments, *déjà vu*, and other insights that we are struggling to explain rationally.[21]

---

[20]Stein, Dan J. *Cognitive Science and the Unconscious* (Arlington, VA: American Psychiatric Publishing, 1997).

[21]Flora, Carlin. "Gut Almighty" *Psychology Today* 40, no. 3 (2007), pp. 68-75.

Neuroscience

As neuroscience now has taken the forefront in understanding the inner workings of human behavior, projects to fully understand the functions of the brain have been launched. *The BRAIN Initiative* (*Brain Research through Advancing Innovative Neurotechnologies*) sponsored by then President Barack Obama was announced in 2013 with a view of acquiring a comprehensive understanding of the brain and its functions, as well as gaining insights into brain disorders and psychological ailments such as depressions and schizophrenia.[22] Also, the European Union has embarked on a similar endeavor, *the Human Brain Project*, aiming to develop an electronic prototype that replicates the human brain.[23] However, one of the key issues that still persists and needs resolution is the mind's subjective experience of the information and perceptions that it acquires and processes, such as the manner in which two persons could describe a color or a particular taste distinctively different, which a computer operating on Boolean logic alone cannot replicate; the so-called 'hard problem' of consciousness, the aforementioned *qualia*.[24] Evidence for a dual process, akin to a conscious and unconscious part working in concert to form holistic human thought patterns have been found in numerous studies, where the different parts of the brain *acti-*

---

[22]The Brain Initiative. https://braininitiative.nih.gov/index.htm (accessed January 1, 2019).

[23]Human Brain Project. https://www.humanbrainproject.eu/ (accessed January 1, 2019).

[24]Graziano, Michael S A. *Consciousness and the Social Brain* (New York: Oxford University Press, 2013).

vate depending on whether associative or analytical thinking are deployed. The right brain hemisphere processes data through unconscious, associative, and automatic thought mechanisms, not in a fragmented manner, but through configured patterns (or in Jungian terms, *archetypes*). It also is not constrained by time or the casual ordering of data. The left-brain hemisphere handles the conscious, cause-effect analytical, and intentional processing of data.[25] There are also efforts within neuroscience to try to combine the findings from 'softer' psychoanalysis in order to better understand the extent of the mind and brain connect. This area of research has been labelled *neuro-psychoanalysis*. There are obviously elements of a cultural clash in attempting to marry these two perspectives, neuroscience with its strictly objective criteria *vis-à-vis* the Freudian-Jungian approach of anecdotal evidence and essay-like descriptions. But by trying to concoct these different views together, the mind-body construct is further elaborated and Freudian concepts could be pinned to specific structures or processes of the brain. Some of the current research areas within neuro-psychoanalysis include:

• defining psychic energy, the libido, as a dopaminergic-seeking system;

• drives or instincts being mapped as emotions with the hypothesis that the brain has seven instinctual networks: seeking; rage; fear; lust;

---

[25]Sternberg, Robert J & Leighton, Jacqueline P. *The Nature of Reasoning* (Cambridge University Press, Cambridge, MA, 2004). p. 300; De Neys, Wim. "Dual processing in reasoning: Two systems but one reasoner." *Psychological Science* 17 (5) 2006, pp. 428-433.

care; panic/grief and play, residing in pontine regions and projecting the cortex, with seeking being constantly active and the others striving for performance as required by the unconscious.[26]

Views of Archetypes

Jung's views of archetypes have gained endorsement from more recent research; in sociobiology, it is assumed that our social conduct has developed through evolution and that it is inherited and affected by natural selection over the generations in the same way it shapes physical features. Socio-biologists and others now believe that humans (and animals) repeat acts that have proved beneficial from an evolutionary point of view, thus advantageous behavior is eventually written into and embedded in the DNA. Therefore, it is possible in certain situations – those relating to evolutionary adaptation and survival – to forecast individual and collective human behavior as they will fall back on these.[27] Additional support for Jung's archetypal proposition comes from *epigenetics*, the study of how individual genes can be activated or deactivated through life experiences and/or the environment. It has been shown that the effects of behavior or events in one lifetime can be genetically passed on to the next generation, causing a sudden 'evolutionary' change. Rather than changing the DNA structure, a specific

---

[26]Schwartz, Casey. "Tell it about your mother – Can brain-scanning help save Freudian psychoanalysis?" *New York Times*. June 28, 2015. http://www.nytimes.com/2015/06/28/magazine/tell-itabout-your-mother.html (accessed January 1, 2019).

[27]Wilson, Edward O. *Sociobiology: The New Synthesis* (Cambridge, MA: Belknap Press of Harvard University Press, 25th Anniversary Edition, 2000).

conduct or event switches on or off particular genes and those genes remain switched on or off in the DNA passed on to the next generation with the capacity to affect both the mental and physical health of the offspring. The study of geographical regions with starvation or other severe environmental conditions has shown that these conditions can cause a change in genes that may be passed on within one generation, something quite contrary to previous perceptions that evolutionary changes take hundreds (or more) of generations to take place.[28]

In his 2012 book, *The Neurobiology of the Gods*, Erik D. Goodwyn examines the most up-to-date evolutionary and cognitive neuroscientific research, seeking a way to understand archetypes in terms of brain physiology.[29] He documents extensive empirical studies that point to a neuroscientific basis for archetypal patterns. However, others, such as Christian Roesler in an article in the *Journal of Analytical Psychology*, "Are Archetypes Transmitted More by Culture Than Biology?" argue that epigenetics in fact raises questions about many of Jung's basic assumptions.[30] New findings in neuroscience provide more and more insight into the functions of the brain and links to the hitherto abstract notion of the mind. While this area of study is still considered a frontier science, regardless of how one chooses to label them, there seems to exist a broad scientific agreement that we have a kind of genetic memory, tendencies

---

[28]Francis, Richard C. *Epigenetics: How Environment Shapes Our Genes* (New York: W.W. Norton & Company, 2012).

[29]Goodwyn, Erik D. *The Neurobiology of the Gods: How Brain Physiology Shapes the Recurrent Imagery of Myth and Dreams* (New York: Routledge, 2012).

[30]Roesler, Christian. *"Are Archetypes Transmitted More by Culture Than Biology?"* Journal of Analytical Psychology 57, no. 2 (2012), pp. 223–246.

for behaviors hard-coded into our DNA that respond in certain ways to certain stimuli. The notion that at birth our mind is a blank slate, *tabula rasa*, has been conclusively discarded and proven erroneous.

CHAPTER 2

WHAT IS THE DEATH DRIVE?

The notion that an innate tendency for self-destruction exists might at first sight seem absurd, how could there be a psychological inclination of that nature as it would completely contradict mankind's resilient will to live? But then again, suicide is amongst the most common forms of death, even extending to collective suicide. A starting point, and an uncontroversial one as such, to understand the possibility of the existence of a self-destructive force must be the acknowledgement that mankind has the ability to override its survival instinct. An assumption which stems from the fact that humans are the only species that become aware early on that life eventually will come to an end. In that sense, self-destructive behavior is merely a way to speed up the inevitable. The prospect of life's end is for most humans a troubling insight and any reflections upon it are generally avoided at great length. It remains an area surprisingly sparsely researched, and suicides and self-inflicted pain are typically associated with mental illness and thus regarded as anomalies.

By reviewing the existing literature and research on self-destructive patterns, commencing with Freud's concept of the death drive, this chapter aims to describe what is known up to now about this ambiguous psychological mechanism.

Sigmund Freud

The Austrian psychologist Sigmund Freud (1856-1939) did *au contraire* to common perceptions not introduce the concept of *Todestrieb*, translated as the *death drive*, in fact, at first, he was somewhat critical of it. However, he examined and reviewed it in his *Beyond the Pleasure Principle* published shortly after World War I, and no doubt the senseless slaughters on the battlefields and in the trenches had made a deep impact on his thinking. From there on, Freud came to be closely linked to the death drive concept and it stands as one of his most controversial theories.[31]

To Freud, the death drive, sometimes also referred to as *Thanatos*, the Greek deity of death, is an intrinsic mental force of the human mind, that together with *Eros*, the life instinct, interacts in a complementary way that forms our behavior. He viewed the death drive as a metaphysical abstract notion, so to tie it to any biological or chemical process of the brain was not possible at the time, and he labelled it a drive, a tendency of sorts, rather than an instinct that acts in a reflex like manner. Whilst *Eros* and *Thanatos* intuitively might appear as opposites, they act

---

[31]Freud, Sigmund, *Beyond the Pleasure Principle*. Translated by C.J.M. Hubback (London, Vienna: Intl. Psycho-analytical, 1922. New York: Bartleby.com, 2010) http://www.bartleby.com/276/ (accessed January 1, 2019).

in conjunction with the aspiration of maintaining a mental equilibrium in accordance with *the nirvana principle*. Freud found evidence for the death drive when he examined patients returning from the war that were suffering from traumatic experiences, something which they often came to re-enact over and over again. Freud concluded that this strange behavior stemmed from the death drive residing in the unconscious, however as these patients only occasionally committed suicide, it appeared that the life instinct often managed to reel in these self-destructive urges. The repetitive patterns were so frequent that they resembled compulsiveness which kept going in the aspiration to seek out an equilibrium in a mindset that had become distorted and tilted. Hence, the death drive operates in a hydraulic fashion, as at some point a certain amount of aggressive forces that have been pent up release, activating a more violent narrative which manifests itself in aggressive behavior and once it has been triggered and repeated often enough, it brings with it a tranquil state of mind, a *catharsis* of sorts. Typically, various civic channels work to redirect this aggressiveness toward more peacefully pursuits; juvenile delinquents are guided into athletics to discharge their aggressions, obviously not always successful and ambivalent adaptions can explain the sometimes unpredictable behaviors of (young) men. Often, however, these feelings are simply repressed or suppressed. The death drive can be directed both outwards as (sadistic) aggression or in a masochistic way be internalized towards self-inflicted pain, extending to suicide.[32]

---

[32]Roazen, Paul, *Freud and His Followers* (New York: Alfred A. Knopf, 1975).

To Freud, much of mankind's history comes down to civilizing and constraining the drives, such as the urges for indolence and sexual expressions. Culture, in its broadest definition, is applied to control these spontaneous expressions to the benefit of solidifying the societal edifice through deliberate planning for long-term survival. As *excessive* spontaneity appears chaotic and might confront the stability of society, norms and morals need to be in place to minimize any inclination to sudden impulsiveness that can lead a civilization astray. This indoctrination, or civilization process, that all societies are confined to as a way to harmonize behavior, must to a degree therefore constrain human drives. If society is not able to acknowledge and allow for acceptable outlets, and the variations of the Roman *"bread and circus"* to appease its population have continued to this day, repression of these urges to the unconscious part of the mind is the only possible way. But ongoing and accumulating repressions are the cause for psychological ailments, including anxiety, as men find difficulties in handling these opposing worldviews from the conscious and unconscious respectively. In essence, to suffer from mental ill-health is, at times, the pre-requisite to be a good citizen as one adheres to and represses what society will not accept, which psychologically means revolting against one's own drives by paying lip service to dogmatic platitudes and slogans. In such an environment, the daily conduct and way of life become over time increasingly artificial, and as society further stagnates psychologically, the degree and frequency of psychological disturbances continue to rise. In hindsight, absurd, even delusional ideas, become *en vogue* and are fully endorsed by the societal in-crowd, subscribing to 'whatever' in order to belong. The rear-view perspective often highlights how detrimental these ideas were, although not recognized as such at the time, and yet how many willing subscribers there were. This moment highlights the advent of the death drive. But the death drive is *per se* never directed towards mankind itself, but rather against a psychologically unhealthy environment. The destructive characteristics of the death drive carry therapeutic properties as it undermines, through a strong psychological impetus, the *status quo*. The revolting actions might be of an unconscious nature at first, such as repeated inadvertent mistakes, miscalculations, covert violations of rules and regulations, but over time become more consciously apparent through cognitive dissonance and subversive affirmations, all of which adds to the chinks in the societal armor, and provide some relief in the quest to regain psychological autonomy. In all, these subversive efforts in aggregate eventually break down the fabrics of society. The mechanism behind the compulsive repetitive patterns therefore provides the opportunity to address the psychological deficiencies accordingly and properly. The elements that have been repressed into the unconscious can in a transcending manner be drawn out and resurface consciously as external perceptions and be addressed as such. But modern psychology rarely takes these constructive, whilst superficially seen as destructive forces positively, as it does not comprehend their underlying motivations and they are therefore seen as something that must remain subdued.

So, a balance is required as to avoid psychological stagnation, where a culture must provide for some level of dynamics as civilizations do and must change over time, so what was frowned upon in the past might be imperative in the future due to changing circumstances. In instances where once repression and sublimation were applied on aggressive tendencies in peace time, these are reverted, relaxed, and even actively encouraged as a country is preparing for war with the risk of engaging in fighting for its very existence.

As Freud analyzed the perpetual conflict between drives and societal demands, he concluded that civilization was founded on a crime, the original *patricide*, hypothesized through his research of the customs and taboos of primitive tribes, and by reconstructing the pre-civilization conditions that formed the origin of cultural advancements. Freud found support for his theories in Charles Darwin's writings that the original man lived in small herds in a dangerous environment, led by a brutal and jealous alpha male protecting his privileges, such as exclusive access to the herd's women. The lives of his sons were tough, if the father became enraged with them, they were either left to fend for themselves or outright murdered. Eventually, the father's tyranny caused a revolt and the sons joined together and killed him. The patricide brought with it split feelings of not only hate and fear, but also a kind of admiration and worship. The murdered father became an authoritative myth and this ambivalent feeling for him led his sons to regret their actions and they established a contract not to kill each other to prevent further murders, and also monogamy was adopted to avoid conflicts over fertile women. These two bans, *not to kill* and *not to commit incest*, were instigated to control mankind's drives of aggression and pleasure that came with the propensity of unleashing unyielding violence that could throw an orderly herd society into disarray. Freud posited that such episodes played out a number of times in individual herds and as these herds merged into bigger communities, extensions and additions to these rules were added and eventually an embryo of a civilization took form. According to Freud, over time institutions were established that codified these behaviors into laws, morals and norms, and also took the form of religion, and could be found in artwork and other cultural manifestations.[33]

Poul Bjerre

An early complementary theory to the death drive was that of the Swedish psychologist Poul Carl Bjerre (1876-1964) who regarded life as evolving around a death and renewal cycle, ideas he published in 1919 prior to Freud's first work on the subject. This recurring cycle is a process that applies both to the individual as well as the collective as over time many aspects of the everyday mundane eventually enter stagnation manifested through repetitive, often lifeless, routines. The necessities of life play an important role in the establishment of such routines which forces humans in various degrees into stagnating mechanistic patterns. If the human mind is not capable of breaking free from these causes of stagnation but becomes stuck in a rut, neurosis can develop. A *psychologic death* then becomes a prerequisite for renewal, if one can succeed in overcoming its transitionary phase and start afresh. It repeats as a continuous cyclic movement between the death phase and the renewal phase as life recurrently drifts back again into *too* repetitive patterns. To Bjerre, this aspiration towards a psychological death originates as seeking a balance and wholeness of the mind, much like Freud's nirvana principle. As such, it is not a self-destructive force, but instead takes aim at eliminating stagnating patterns in life that risk mental fatigue and inertia. At the collective level, it can be diagnosed as the last and terminal phase of a dogmatic culture whose contents have been

---

[33]Freud, Sigmund, *Civilization and Its Discontents* (London: Penguin, 2002).

driven to excess and triggered societal stagnation, where tired platitudes and slogans are parroted representing dogmatic beliefs detached
from reality, and now completely lacking the ardor and intensity to stir
genuine emotions. And as the obstinate repressive environment has allowed for an ever-increasing number of taboos to dictate and diminish
the plethora of opinions, as it lingers on it will suffocate human initiatives by further constraining any acceptable outlets where it can perform. A general behavior of neurosis becomes prevalent in society,
marked by scapegoating and witch hunts, and has the capacity of triggering violence with revolutions and wars as manifestations of collective death, which then will come to the mark the start of psychological
renewal.[34]

Carl Gustav Jung

The Swiss psychologist Carl Gustav Jung (1875-1961) defined a sort
of collective psychological thought patterns, *archetypes*, that reside in the
unconscious part of the mind and acts as influencing forces on human
behavior. These archetypes, finite in numbers, representing various aspects of human life, including birth and death, are a kind of fall back
collective psychological patterns, normally residing dormant in the unconscious, to which mankind reverts to in situations where a particular
psychological make-up is warranted and thus a suitable archetype is activated. Archetypes bring with them ideas and views that starkly contrast with the reigning distorted culture and hold persuading powers
that are difficult to shut down, and they eventually emerge into the conscious, in what is referred to as *integration of the unconscious*, holding an

---

[34]Bjerre, Poul Carl, *Death and Renewal* (New York: MacMillan, 1930).

important function in ensuring psychological well-being. In that sense, the new archetype brings with it a narrative that better aligns with the changing realities.[35]

As an archetype activates to rectify a psychological imbalance, it replaces an active but faltering archetype that cannot address the situation but once was triggered to deal with some preceding psychological problem and formed a narrative with context composed fixed thought patterns. Hence, the previous archetype becomes dormant again, transcending back to the unconscious part of the mind. In a sense, this transition represents the death and birth of specific psychological content rather than the generic psychological force that the Freudian death drive represents. However, the manifestations are much the same; addressing a psychological imbalance in dire need of a correction.

Jung shared Freud's view that in neurosis there are two psychological tendencies in conflict, one that wants to repress and another seeking freedom. And like Freud, he concluded that human drives tend to clash with the normative constraints and morals that society imposes. In Jung's words:

---

[35]Jung, C.G., *The Archetypes and the Collective Unconscious* translated by R.F.C. Hull, 2nd ed (Princeton, New Jersey: Princeton University Press, 1981) p. 87-110.

'We also know today that it is by no means the animal nature alone that is at odds with civilized constraints; very often it is new ideas which are thrusting upwards from the unconscious and are just as much out of harmony with the dominating culture as the instincts. For instance, we could easily construct a political theory of neurosis...'[36]

However, it is generally not obvious for a community or society at large that its attitudes and norms have become skewed in a way that might lead to mental illnesses, given that they often are so caught up and formed by the reigning normative values. Therefore, the activation of archetypes to address psychological deficiencies might appear spontaneous once they have entered awareness and their physical manifestations can be observed, albeit generally only in hindsight. This makes it difficult to forecast which archetype that will arise and when exactly it will activate. It is worthwhile to note that the unconscious attitudes will not always contrast with the dominant conscious mindset but they can also take a more complementary form. Thus, one cannot automatically project an opposing polarized psychological reaction to an existing mentally imbalanced environment. The appearance of the archetype's corresponding symbolic manifestations will indicate their character and content.

Jung stated that when the mind starts working on restoring equilibrium through activating an archetype, the outlet of the archetypal activation itself is likely to lead to behaviors with *pathological* characteris-

---

[36]Jung, C. G., *Two Essays on Analytical Psychology* translated by R.F.C. Hull, 2nd ed (Princeton, New Jersey: Princeton University Press, 1977) p. 20.

tics.[26] This would include various types of erratic and neurotic behaviors that when appearing in societal situations could, depending on the magnitude of the force of the archetypal energy, span from obsessions to noticeably bizarre and odd fads and trends that suddenly seem to appear from nowhere, to the abrupt flare-up of civil unrests, demonstrations, riots, revolutions, and even war. Regardless of the rationale for archetypes to activate, the process is essentially a transformation, where a slumbering archetype is brought out and assimilated into the collective conscious' disposition. This means that already from activation in the unconscious until the embedding into the collective conscious, the archetypes will exert an influence on human actions and behaviors.

An additionally important characteristic is that archetypes are neither a negative nor a positive force. The activation of an archetype with aggressive characteristics need not necessarily be viewed as negative but can be triggered as a psychological force to restore a society dominated by apathetic attitudes and lethargy, although the consequences of activating such an archetype might well lead to increased violent displays in society. As the archetype is a dynamic autonomous agent that directs our actions in ways of which we initially are not aware of or can consciously control, it becomes, on a collective basis, difficult to break or diverge from its influence once it has activated.

Perspectives of Freud's drive theory

The theories of human drives, or instincts, have older roots than Freud, the more formalized versions commence with Charles Darwin's theory of evolution in the mid-nineteenth century. The psychologists

William James (1842-1910) and William McDougall (1871-1938) provided taxonomies of instincts that were considered to regulate various human behaviors. Freud in a sense brought all these together into two drives; *Eros* and *Thanatos* that operate in conjunction through a dynamic system. The energy fueling this system, the *libido*, is the source that directs different behaviors as it flows around in the human mind accordingly. However, Freud himself was never certain whether the libido was something abstract, i.e. simply a metaphor, or if it existed as a chemical substance.[37][38]

Typically to many of Freud's psychoanalytical concepts, his views on them kept changing over the years and the death drive was no exception. In his time, the death drive was received with skepticism, and the fact that Freud kept changing his opinion on it did nothing to help gain acceptance for the concept. To his disciples and neo-Freudians, it has remained among the most controversial of his theories and came to a degree to undermine the popularity of psychoanalysis itself, especially post-World War II. As with so many other concepts in psychoanalysis, a lot came down to the fact that it was not possible to verify and objectively test, but rather the theories relied on anecdotal evidence and case studies. The notion of a death drive did not come down well with the political sentiments that reigned after the massacres and bloodshed of World War II, especially with the existence of a weapon of mass destruction, the atomic bomb. Speaking of a death drive was no longer *comme-*

---

[37]Buss, David M., *Evolutionary psychology: the new science of the mind* (New York: Psychology Press, 2014) Chapter 1.

[38]McDougall, William, *An Introduction to Social Psychology* 2nd ed. (London, United Kingdom: Methuen & Co, 1909).

il-faut and the community of psychologists sought a more positive approach with nurture rather than nature dominating the characteristics of mankind. With more liberal, and to some extent Freudo-Marxist, views of the world, biological determinism was dismissed, as focus now was on various pro-active methods to improve the psychological well-being, in particular through education and medication. Also, the practical applications of a death drive remained unclear to psychologists. What could they actually do with it?

However, even as the death drive concept fell in disarray, some of Freud's disciples carried the torch and developed it further, amongst them, the Austrian psychoanalyst Melanie Klein (1882-1960) that expanded on its definition. To Klein, and unlike Freud, it is the fear of death itself that is the root cause of all anxiety. In that sense, the death drive is viewed as a drive to destroy, rather than Freud's view that it is a complementary psychological force to Eros. Klein based these theories from her clinical research of analyzing children's fantasies and noted the many cruel aspects and details they contained. Such cruelties could not be explained through experience, as the children simply were too young, so she concluded and concurred with Freud that it must be an innate force, a drive which we are born with, but she interpreted its characteristics more negatively.[39]

The German psychologist Erich Fromm (1900-1980) spent part of his career studying Freud's work, mainly criticizing what he saw as inconsistencies in Freud's description of the human mind's two main forces manifested through desire and repression. Fromm maintained

---

[39]Segal, Hanna, *Introduction to the Work of Melanie Klein* (London, United Kingdom: Karnac Books, 1988).

that Freud and later disciples never fully clarified these differing forces. Despite denouncing some of Freud's work, he also was inspired by him and wrote extensively on the collective aspects of neurosis and pathology, and what is and is not normality. In *The Sane Society* from 1955, being among his most famous works, Fromm commented from a Marxist perspective and argued that the capitalist system with its free market and the focus on consumption and materialism would lead to a commoditization of man that would drive citizens towards neurosis and other psychological conditions. He tried to define in detail what makes a society 'sick' and when what is seen as normal becomes psychologically hurtful for mankind. However, on the psychological effects of Marxist materialism and the *Lysenkoism* approach to create and homogenize the socialist man, Fromm was notably silent.[40]

He pointed out that what is considered normal shifts over time, and the fact that even if a majority of the population supports certain ideas or habitual patterns that does not prove them psychologically sound. As an example, Fromm saw a greedy society as an insane society and if its population participates in greedy behavior and excessive consumerism, it produces a pathological normality. The effect will be that under this normality, humans will suffer psychologically and such a society will see a great number of cases of neurosis and anxiety as *healthy* reactions against these conditions. He referred to Freud in his conclusion:

---

[40]Fromm, Erich, *The Sane Society* 2nd ed (New York: Routledge, 2014) Chapter 2.

That human nature and society can have conflicting demands, and hence that a whole society can be sick, is an assumption which was made very explicitly by Freud, most extensively in his Civilization and Its Discontents.[41]

He pointed to not only the past but that also the future prospects of civilization being in danger of mass psychosis: *"I believe we have every right to speak of a 'mentally ill society'... If society generally produces people suffering from grave schizophrenia, it will endanger its very existence."* This role of psychopathology in society has since been shared by a number of psychoanalysts and cultural critics.[42]

The German philosopher Herbert Marcuse (1898-1979) wrote in his *Eros and Civilization: A Philosophical Inquiry into Freud* from 1955 that he disagreed with Freud's pessimism regarding the possibility of ever erasing the conflict between Eros and the death drive, and argued that civilization could be radically transformed in an erotic direction, such that the death drive could be tamed or pacified by Eros. His views came to some extent to shape the radical ideas of the 1960s, including the idea of 'free love,' however history has since refuted much of Marcuse's theories.[43]

Ludvig Igra, (1945-2003) the Polish-Swedish psychoanalyst spent much of his career pondering over the death drive. Highlighted in his 1988 book *På liv och död: om destruktivitet och livsvilja,* Igra saw the death

[41]Ibid, p. 19.

[42]Ibid, Chapter 2.

[43]Marcuse, Herbert, *Eros and Civilization: A Philosophical Inquiry into Freud* (Boston, MA: Beacon Press, New ed., 1974).

drive triggered from traumatic experiences, which generally are inevitable parts of the human development. The traumatization led to 'toxic' feelings forming, and with toxic Igra refers to emotions that cannot be endured but must be projected externally, often finding scapegoats to harbor these. The death drive can, according to Igra, be regarded as an unconscious flow of phantasies with a specific structure as source, i.e. the theme that is likely to be projected, and out of these phantasies stem perceptions, internal conflicts, and patterns of action.[44] He concurred with Freud's view that the death drive and Eros are general tendencies in our mind sharing the same objective – namely to avoid inner mental conflicts but that they operate in different fashions. Eros seeks to preserve life through creating ever more coupled and integrated units of wholeness. The death drive, on the other hand, seeks to divide, dissolve and destroy.[45]

The Slovenian psychoanalytical philosopher Slavoj Žižek argues that the death drive is a primary psychological force, such that in order to risk our own lives in war or to decide to have offspring, there must be an unconscious belief, at least, of our own immortality, whether that is of our souls having eternal values or the passing of our genes to the next generation. As such, Žižek subscribes to a biological determinism of sorts so that man will aspire, and sometimes being unaware of these ulterior motives, to create cultural institutions, including ideology and religion that sustain these perpetual ambitions. To Žižek, what the Freudian theorem comes down to is a battle between the conscious part

---

[44]Igra, Ludvig, *På liv och död: Om destruktivitet och livsvilja* (Lund, Sweden: Studentlitteratur AB, 2003) pp. 31-33.

[45]Ibid, pp. 43-44.

of the mind, and the drives, where the conscious part attempts to seek control over human action, but in fact it is the drives that lead.[46]

Repression versus Suppression

Freud and Freudians wrote extensively about the processes which excluded the parts of reality not deemed suitable for the societal morals and norms, the defense mechanisms. Their typical function is to protect the conscious part of the mind from unwelcomed perceptions that will not corroborate with the acceptable, and as such they are directed into the unconscious. However, if they are allowed to linger on in ever increasing numbers, they can trigger neurosis. The capacity of the unconscious part of the mind to absorb a considerably larger amount of perceptions than what can be consciously digested has been verified through a number of empirical studies.[47] Out of the many defense mechanisms, it is, in the context of the death drive, important to distinguish between *repressions* and *suppressions* as they are sometimes incorrectly being used interchangeably:

Repression: an impulse that forces something emotionally painful to be forgotten and consigned to the unconscious. Because the psychological issue has not been dealt with or resolved by the conscious part

---

[46]Hook, Derek, *Of Symbolic Mortification and 'Undead Life': Slavoj Žižek on the Death Drive*. Psychoanalysis and History, Volume 18 Issue 2, 2016, pp. 221-256 http://www.euppublishing.com/doi/abs/10.3366/pah.2016.0190?journalCode=pah (accessed January 1, 2019).

[47]Freud, Anna, *The Ego and the Mechanisms of Defense* (London, United Kingdom; Karnac Books, 1992).

of the mind, it continues to affect the person unconsciously and can eventually develop into mental disorders;

Suppression: a conscious act to forget something in an attempt to cope with a troubling situation. As suppression only pushes stressful thoughts or emotions into the preconscious part of the mind, as such it is relatively easy to retrieve them later and work on accepting or resolving them.

In essence, repression is the unconscious avoidance of threatening information whereas suppression is a consciously deliberate avoidance of the same.[48]

The existence of defense mechanisms, in particular repression and suppression, where perceptions not in congruence with acceptable norms are coerced below the surface of awareness, have been acknowledged through more recent studies. Research points to a link between psychical ailments and a repressive personality, i.e. persons with a tendency to avoid expressing emotions either intentionally or unconsciously when dealing with situations of distress by suppressing/repressing them.[49] Manifestations like neurosis and depressions are the

---

[48]Ibid.

[49]Schwartz, C. *Tell it about your mother – Can brain-scanning help save Freudian psychoanalysis*. New York Times, June 24, 2015. http://www.nytimes.com/2015/06/28/magazine/tell-itabout-your-mother.html?_r=0 (accessed January 1, 2019).

bodily symptoms from the unconscious that the conscious part of the mind cannot verbally formalize.[50]

The Death Drive Today

The South African psychoanalyst Mark Solms has presented a theory on affect regulation (in Freudian parlance drives), claiming that they function to make us aware of psychological imbalances in need of addressing. Based on the fact that we can only store a limited amount of information in our conscious part of the mind, about 6-8 bits, much of our behavior needs to be automated to keep as many perceptions as possible outside our conscious, given its scarce memory resources. This notion differs from Freud's view of the unconscious as a dustbin for repressed perceptions, to Solms the unconscious is also about not overloading the conscious part of the mind.[51]

Solms refers to *set points*, a sort of psychological equilibriums that constitute the ideal status for our drives, if we deviate from them, a sense of anxiety or psychological commotions occur. Negative emotions make us aware that we are moving away from the equilibrium and positive emotions emerge when we are returning towards it. These set points are, in accordance with Freud's theories, holistic principles of

---

[50]Garssen, B. December 2007. *Repression: Finding our way in the maze of concepts.* Journal of Behavioral Medicine 30 (6). http://www.ncbi.nlm.nih.gov/pmc/articles/PMC 2080858/ (accessed January 1, 2019) pp. 471-481.

[51]Solms, Mark, *The Neuropsychology of Dreams: A Clinico-anatomical Study* (Institute for Research in Behavioral Neuroscience Series) (New York: Psychology Press, 1st ed, 2015).

seeking mental well-being.[52] Solms links it to our ability to learn how to control and overcome emotions in order to return to these set points through designated actions. Emotions also indicate erroneous projections that we have automated and kept outside the conscious part of the mind. Hence, in such cases, we must then recalibrate our cognitive abilities to make better projections which then again can be automated. If these operate adequately, no emotions will appear. But less efficient behavior also gets automated, and these will emerge as we deviate from the set points. These findings come close to the Freudian notion of a repressed unconscious that keeps resurfacing and according to Solms, psychological unhealthiness relates to erroneous behaviors and solutions that operate and act against our drives and it is this urge to constantly try to automate behavior that tends to sometimes lead us astray psychologically. Negative emotions and an aspiration to undo and eliminate these behaviors align with the Freudian death drive concept and can also be applied on *erroneous* mental patterns formed by collective narratives and norms.[53]

Solms's views that there are biological explanations to a psychological mechanism akin to the death drive and repressions as an affiliated defense mechanism have in parts been echoed by the Israeli neuro-psychoanalyst Efrat Ginot, highlighted in her 2015 book, *The Neuropsychology of The Unconscious*. Ginot points out how the brain, due to efficiency efforts, constantly seeks to automate our actions and behaviors with the effect that it develops a number of automated processes, in part or

---

[52]Ibid.

[53]Ibid.

wholly unconscious. This, as Solms mentioned, is done due to the conscious part of the mind's size constraints, hence plenty of perceptions need to be re-routed to the unconscious, in that sense a death drive-like force operates to adjust and to erase faulty automated behaviors and to create a more viable psychological mindset, also at the collective level.[54]

From a neuroscientific point of view, we know that the right part of the brain provides implicit processes, implicit memory, cognitions and affect. These processes are fast (250-500 milliseconds), unconscious, non-verbal, and automatic in nature. The right part processes information assembled through unity structures, such as *gestalt,* and all information is presented simultaneously, complexed and synthetic in the present. The left part of the brain provides explicit processes, which are slower, conscious, verbal, and deliberate. It operates in a serial and logical fashion to provide a sense of control within the constraints of language. It can only handle information in the past and thoughts about the future, and can in principle only deliver information about what we already know. On the other hand, the right half of the brain is not constrained by formal logic and sequential ordering but can perceive

---

[54]Ginot, Efrat, *The Neuropsychology of the Unconscious: Integrating Brain and Mind in Psychotherapy* (Norton Series on Interpersonal Neurobiology) (New York: W.W. Norton & Company, 1st ed, 2015).

unique objects and phenomena through association. It is considered to be the base for our emotional and social skills.[55, 56, 57]

The repression and suppression defense mechanisms are found in various acts of self-deception, which is a process of either denying or rationalizing away logical arguments that contradict a subscribed belief or value, whether those have been imposed upon or self-obtained. Reality is misinterpreted, in particular the perceptions of one's own relation to reality. It is often done to convince oneself of a certain view of reality that has turned into a dogma, much like an unquestionable truth. Part of this self-deception might occur unconsciously (repression) so any awareness of them are not obvious. These periods of self-deception can last long and often with severe consequences, as perceptions of reality tends to become skewed and misaligned. And by truncating reality and omitting parts of it, eventually irrational behavior enters, meaning that a lot of decision-making will operate on paradoxes. For some, this can eventually become overwhelming and psychological disturbances can develop, much in the way Freud described the manifests of the

---

[55]Goel, V., Bruchel, C., Frith, C., Dolan, R. *Dissociation of mechanisms underlying syllogistic reasoning* NeuroImage 2000, 12 (5). https://www.ncbi.nlm.nih.gov/pubmed/11034858 (accessed January 1, 2019), pp. 504-514.

[56]Goel, V., Dolan, R., *Explaining modulation of reasoning by belief* Cognition 2003, 87 (1) http://www.sciencedirect.com/science/article/pii/S0010027702001853? via%3 Dihub (accessed January 1, 2019), pp. B11-B22.

[57]Stupple, E., Waterhouse, E.F., *Negations in syllogistic reasoning: Evidence for a heuristic–analytic conflict* The Quarterly Journal of Experimental Psychology 2009, 62(8). http://www.tandfonline.com/doi/abs/10.1080/17470210902785674 (accessed January 1, 2019), pp.1533-1541.

death drive.[58] Some of these psychological disturbances can evolve into self-destructive behavior, including actions to engage in self-harm. This can include a wide array of manifestation from mutilating oneself to various forms of substance abuse, eating disorders, and ultimately successful or unsuccessful suicide attempts. One can expose oneself to adverse lifestyles and thought patterns that will lead in the direction of abuse, exploitations and pain whether of a physical or psychological sort. Often such behavior is referred to as low self-esteem or self-despise, however it fits with the description of the death drive. But self-destructive tendencies can also be willfully adapted in order to bow out of situations one realizes, if only implicitly, that one cannot handle, by triggering anxiety or the feeling of unworthiness and thus inadvertently starting to self-sabotage, for instance neglecting one's preparations for an exam, an athletic competition, or an important career project, by in various ways highlighting incompetence and unsuitability, with the consequence that the expectations of performance are being lowered.[59] Obviously, one needs to distinguish dedicated efforts to end one's life from deliberate self-harm, including intentionally failed suicide attempts, where the latter does not seek such an outcome, hence often labelled *non-suicidal self-injury*. The current view in psychology is that

---

[58]McLaughlin, Brian P., Oksenberg Rorty, Amélie, *Perspectives on Self-Deception (Topics in Philosophy)* (Berkeley and Los Angeles, California: University of California Press, 1988).

[59]Johnston, Mark, *Self-Deception and the Nature of Mind Philosophy of Psychology: Debates on Psychological Explanation* Philosophy of Psychology (Debates on Psychological Explanation) (Cambridge, United Kingdom: Blackwell Publishing, 1995), pp. 63-91.

these are seen as coping mechanisms to regulate anxiety and other associated psychological ailments in order to avoid unpleasant situations, emotions, and thoughts.[60] Of course, these types of self-injuries can often have legitimate root cause stemming from abuse, such as of an emotional and sexual nature, or various traumas.[61, 62] It has also been demonstrated that self-harm acts as an aspiration to replace feeling of nothingness with pain just to make one feel alive, and as such, it can trigger repetitive patterns and the urge for this pain becomes an addiction, again much resembling how Freud described the compulsiveness of the death drive.[63]

[60]Näslund, Görel Kristina, *Borderline personlighetsstörning: Uppkomst, symptom, behandling, prognos* (Stockholm, Sweden: Natur och kultur, 1998), pp. 108-111.

[61]Meltzer, Howard, et al., *Non Fatal Suicidal Behaviour Among Adults aged 16 to 74, Great Britain* (London, United Kingdom: National Statistics The Stationery Office, 2000) http://webarchive.nationalarchives.gov.uk/ 20160128193136/ http://www.ons.gov.uk/ons/rel/psychiatric-morbidity/ non-fatal-suicidal-behaviour-among-adults/aged-16-74-in-great-britain/ index.html (accessed January 1, 2019).

[62]Rea, K., Aiken, F., Borastero, C., "Building Therapeutic Staff: Client Relationships with Women who Self-Harm." *Women's Health Issues* 1997, 7 (2). http://www.whijournal.com/article/S1049-3867(96)00112-0/pdf (accessed January 1, 2019) pp. 121-125.

[63]Kaba, Fatos, et al., "Solitary Confinement and Risk of Self-Harm Among Jail Inmates." *American Journal of Public Health,* March 2014, 104 (3). http://ajph.aphapublications.org/doi/pdf/10.2105/ AJPH.2013.301742 (accessed January 1, 2019) pp. 442-447.

Conclusions

Whilst Freud's notion of a death drive was downplayed after his demise, concepts analogous to it kept emerging, obscured through differing terminology but recognizable through its shared manifestations. Notably, the repression and suppression of perceptions deemed inappropriate have shown to cause psychological ailments, often with displays of aggression either acted out or manifested through self-harm as a means of attempting to alter an unhealthy psychological environment. Neuroscientific evidence points to mental phenomena comparable to the death drive, but the term is rarely used today, possibly the name itself comes across as too dramatic, however its meaning as Freud posited it is applied as disparate concepts by contemporary psychology.

THE PSYCHOLOGY OF THE COLLECTIVE

Will a collective respond to psychological stimuli similarly to the way an individual would, and, for the purpose of this book, can a society, or even a distinct culture and civilization, be influenced by the death drive? Is it possible for a society to emerge on a path of self-destruction where it collectively walks into its own demise with eyes wide open? While mass suicides have been known for millennia, typically they have been a preferred last resort, to avoid capture by bloodthirsty enemies, while others occur in a religious context where a frenzy has been worked up in which a premature entrance into an after-world paradise has become the desired path to avoid perdition. However, one needs to distinguish between mass suicide and the death drive which operates on a different psychological impetus.

In that sense, are collectively self-destructive patterns, with the implicit objective of eradicating civic institutions that no longer serve its citizens' psychological well-being and with a view to replacing them with something more advantageous, viable?

The Freudian Perspective

Freud took inspiration from the French polymath Gustave Le Bon (1841-1931) who published one of the most influential works on crowd psychology *The Crowd: A Study of the Popular Mind* in 1895, and concluded that a concept of a group mind would operate through the same mental processes as the individual mind.[64] Freud referred to a *racial unconscious* to be added to his theories of a repressed unconscious which was a shared cultural and genetic psychological vessel that carried common contents at the unconscious level.[65]

Freud hypothesized that the death drive concept also could embrace groups and social formations and suggested that the innate aggression within a group can be directed towards other collectives or used to eliminate any internal opposition. In *Group Psychology and the Analysis of the Ego* from 1921, he stated:

> ...*only rarely and under certain exceptional conditions is individual psychology in a position to disregard the relations of the individual to others. In the individual's mental life someone else is invariably involved ...individual psychology is at the same time social psychology.*[66]

---

[64]Freud, Sigmund. *Totem and Taboo, Some Points of Agreement between the mental Lives of Savages and Neurotics* (London: Routledge & Kegan Paul, 1950) p. 157.

[65]Freud, Sigmund. *Beyond the Pleasure Principle, Group Psychology and Other Works* In Standard Edition, XVIII (1920-1922). (London: Hogarth, 1955) p. 75.

[66]Freud, Sigmund. *Group Psychology and the Analysis of the Ego* (London, Vienna: The International Psychoanalytical Press, 1922) Chapter 1.

To Freud, social relationships were an important component in understanding an individual's psychology. As mentioned in the previous chapter, he saw the first impulses to the development of a society originating from the bans on murder and incest which stemmed from the desires to curb aggression and libido because if these are allowed free reign, civilization is at risk:

> *The first form of social organization came about with a renunciation of instincts, a recognition of mutual obligations, the introduction of definite institutions, pronounced inviolable (holy) – that is to say, the beginnings of morality and justice. Each individual renounced his ideal of acquiring his father's position for himself and of possessing his mothers and sisters. Thus, the taboo on incest and the injunction to exogamy came about.[67]*

Civilizations were established through agreeing to these bans amongst a group of leaders that through sheer brute force could impose them on the rest of the population as they sought to hold a monopoly on violence. It is when the power of the collective replaces the power of individuals that the first step towards establishing a civilization commences but that is at the expense of its individual members that, implicitly at least, agree to cease control over their urges to aggression and libidinous desires by conforming through repressing and suppressing them.

---

[67]Freud, Sigmund. *Moses and Monotheism* (New York: Martino Fine Books 2010 reprint, 1939) p. 82.

Freud also highlighted that the psychology of the crowd tends to supersede the psychology of the individual. Among other ideas described in his 1930s work *Civilization and Its Discontents*, is that belonging to a crowd allows for the unconscious part of the mind to be accessed. This is due to the moral constraints of the individual being reconfigured by surrendering to a greater collective under the control of an authoritarian leadership. Freud argued that what holds the collective together is a fear by individuals of being alone and their anxiety about risking separation from the herd is, on average, stronger than any opposition to repressive norms.[68, 69, 70]

The Jungian Perspective

To Freud, a group mind was led by the unconscious, a view he shared with Le Bon. Jung however, was adamant that both the collective conscious and collective unconscious formed the discourse that governs and steers the group and its world view. He argued that the collective conscious part of the mind forms public opinion, being a distillation of the average person's cultural and moral values into a set of societal beliefs, norms, attitudes, and mainstream political -*isms*, such as socialism,

---

[68]Gay, Peter. *Freud: A Life for Our Time* (London: W W Norton & Co Inc, 1989), p. 547.

[69]Freud, Sigmund. *Civilization and Its Discontents*. In Civilization, Society and Religion (London: W W Norton & Co Inc, 1987) p. 311.

[70]Jones, Ernest. *The Life and Work of Sigmund Freud* (London: Pelican Books, 1964), p. 508.

liberalism, fascism, or communism, depending on the prevailing context. The values held in the collective conscious tend to be shared among the greater majority of individuals in the group, and these generally supersede any conflicting personal beliefs or values. And as an individual can suffer from psychological ailments, so can the collective, and both Freud and Jung noted the existence of collective psychological disorders, such as traumas and neurosis. Jung pointed to archetypal influences at work, albeit only anecdotal, in the decline of the Roman Empire and the French Revolution.[71]

Jung even attempted to create a political theory based on collective neurosis, albeit it remained at an embryonic stage, through studying human excitement triggered by political passions, no doubt he reflected on the totalitarian movements of the 1920s and 1930s.[72] He suggested that as contents in the unconscious became psychically charged and volatile as a consequence of them being repressed, they eventually resurfaced into awareness in the form of various cults, crazes, crudities, and in the modern era as political ideologies.[73]

---

[71]Jung, C.G. *On the Nature of the Psyche* (Vol. 8 of The Collected Works of C. G. Jung), trans. R.F.C. Hull, 2nd ed. (Princeton, NJ: Princeton University Press, 1981), par. 435.

[72]Jung, C.G., *Collected Works of C.G. Jung, Volume 7: Two Essays in Analytical Psychology* (New Jersey: Princeton University Press, 1967) p. 19

[73]Odajnyk Walter V. *Jung and Politics: The Political and Social Ideas of C. G. Jung* (Lincoln, NE: Authors Choice Press, 2007) Chapter 5.

Internally, they give rise to personal neuroses and psychoses; exter-
nally, their malevolent force may appear in spectacular crime-assas-
sination, for example. In most people, however, the repressed energy
'remains in the background, and only manifests itself indirectly in
the inexorable moral degeneration of society.[74]

However, Jung's claim should not be taken such that all populist movements are ultimately a product of psychological afflictions, but it does mean that as long as contents and perceptions need to be repressed to the unconscious *en masse*, these often provoke conflicts that on the surface appear to be purely political. The repression of aggressive tendencies leads to a sense of anxiety and guilt, also at the collective level, and then frequently, and inadvertently at first, encourage hostility and violence that subverts society and triggers rebellion.[75, 76]

Zeitgeist

Zeitgeist is a German word that broadly translates as *"the spirit of the age"* and is a somewhat elusive concept that provides a narrative and context to the overall cultural, political, intellectual, mood sentiments, and/or moral ambience for the particular time époque and collective

---

[74]Jung, C.G., *Collected Works of C.G. Jung, Volume 7: Two Essays in Analytical Psychology* (New Jersey: Princeton University Press, 1967) par. 150.

[75]Odajnyk Walter V. *Jung and Politics: The Political and Social Ideas of C. G. Jung* (Lincoln, NE: Authors Choice Press, 2007) chapter 5.

[76]Jung, C. G. *Collected Works of C.G. Jung, Volume 7: Two Essays in Analytical Psychology* (New Jersey: Princeton University Press, 1967) par. 152.

group. Certain fixed ideas or themes will come to exist within the zeitgeist. These fixations become an embedded part of the collective's perception of reality, they start to trigger action and behaviors to synchronize and align with the gist of the zeitgeist. So, what in retrospect might appear to have been absurd statements or decisions made by someone while seized by the zeitgeist were in fact highly rational under the rigorous context and thought pattern dictated by it. They seem to govern which reality to focus on and what to consciously disregard but nevertheless is unconsciously registered; in other words, turning a blind eye to features of reality or considering reality from a heavily skewed perception. This is the power of the zeitgeist, the discrepancies between psychological illusions that perceive reality, leading to a refusal to observe what is in front of us.[77, 78]

And if elements of reality do not corroborate with the world view provided by the zeitgeist, these are ignored or distorted and interpreted not to conflict with the reigning narrative. However, if these elements become too overwhelming and seem to threaten the foundation societal values, the elements cannot only be frowned upon by a conformist public but even be declared "illegal knowledge."

Why does the zeitgeist then not stay the same? Over time, norms have a tendency to become fixated into rigid formality in which the original purpose of the norm and psychological balance they were set to ensure no longer can be met, i.e. more aspects of reality are filtered out

[77]Magee, G.A. *Zeitgeist, The Hegel Dictionary* (London, United Kingdom: Continuum International Publishing Group, 2011) p. 262.

[78]von Franz, M.-L *Archetypal Dimensions of the Psyche* (Boston, MA: Shambala Publications Inc., 1999) pp. 263-285.

not to confront the conformity of the zeitgeist, they hence no longer fulfil their original purpose, and over time fall in disarray.

Taboos

Taboos are defined as items relating to human activities that are prohibited or strongly condemned based on the reigning societal or moral and religious convictions. In the Victorian era, the noted taboo was anything related to sexuality. As a rule of thumb, taboos are identified through the strong reactions to particular words or a theme triggering heated emotions. Another example is the swift change of discussion topic or other typical displacement activities that signal a disturbance in response to a taboo, or the use of euphemisms to neutralize its contentiousness. Taboos dictate the public discourse, what can and cannot be debated, often seen as items considered inappropriate by what today is labelled as political correctness. What is considered taboo changes over time and will differ depending on cultural contexts. There seems to be very few items that are perpetually seen as taboo, or at least the scope of a certain taboo can vary widely.[79]

What is then the difference between taboos and norms? One interpretation is that taboos are strong norms; norms that are sufficiently strong so that they may be viewed as sacred and breaching them will be castigated through severe social sanctions. But the implications of taboo are wider than just being considered a more extreme form of norms,

---

[79]Encyclopædia Britannica Online. *Taboo*. Encyclopædia Britannica Inc. 2012. http://global.britannica.com/topic/taboo-sociology (accessed January 1, 2019).

taboos are sometimes referred to as the *'unthinkable.'* Even thinking about violating a taboo becomes problematic. Under this interpretation, a taboo is a form of a censor on thinking and in that sense, taboos exist to prevent unconscious impulses from manifesting.[80]

Later developments

From a contemporary perspective, the collective unconscious and zeitgeist are terms rarely used, but rather psychologists and sociologists refer to *collective mental states*, however its definition bears noted similarities with the definitions of the now antiquated vocabulary, and this shifting labelling makes for confusion in finding a red thread when studying historical documents and trying to tie them to current settings.

To analyze a society, its collective psychological variations need to be established, in particular the notion of a collective mind which incorporates a collective conscious and is underpinned by a collective memory. This collective memory is shaped by certain reminiscences, whether correctly represented or not, that are selected as 'true' representations of history, a memory bias is at play here, which forms a narrative (zeitgeist) that provides a shared perspective on the outlook not only of history but also of the present and future. Jung's concept of the collective unconscious has in modern times been expanded on, and is now often re-labelled as a *social unconscious*, referring to the existence and constraints of social, cultural and communicational arrangements

---

[80]Tetlock, PE; Orie, KV; Elson, B; Green, MC; Lerner, JS. *The psychology of the unthinkable: Taboo trade-offs, forbidden base rates, and heretical counterfactuals* Journal of Personality and Social Psychology 2000, 78 (5): 853-870. http://www.ncbi.nlm. nih.gov/pubmed/10821194 (accessed January 1, 2019)

of which people are unaware, in the sense of not being explicitly acknowledged.[81] Instead of the Jungian archetypes, references are made to shared anxieties, traumas and fantasies which typically are arranged by certain themes.[82]

Types of Collective Mental States

To apply the death drive concept on a collective, the span of the various mental states needs to be defined, in particular drawing a delineation between balanced and unbalanced mental states as it is in the latter that a death drive is presumed to activate. Various collective mental states have been described throughout history and some appear linked to certain cultures, such as the Portuguese *Saudade* and the German *Sehnsucht*, describing a melancholy of sorts, even lingering towards depression. From a psychiatric perspective, a mentally ill society can be gauged through the shifting and trending numbers of psychological illnesses and patients. Albeit the measurement problems are obvious as there is a stigma associated with them so underreporting is a noted problem but also the definitions of mental ailments differ over time, as do the resources to identify and remedy these.

Some of the collective modes include:

---

[81]Hopper, Earl. *The social unconscious: Theoretical considerations* Group Analysis. Special Issue 34, 2001, (1): 9-27.

[82]Weinberg, Haim. *So What is this Social Unconscious Anyway?* Group Analysis. Volume 40, Issue 3, 2007.

Collective fear, or collective paranoia, has by some been pointed out as a causal factor in genocides and ethnic cleansing.[83]

Collective traumas and collective depressions share similarities; however, the former is typically abruptly triggered. A traumatic event, such as a massacre or the assassination of a political statesman can ignite a collective psychological sentiment with noted shifts in culture and politics, and with the propensity of prompting mass movements which can last over generations.[84] Individual depressions caused by such an event can be so common that the actual numbers form the impression of a collective epidemic and, *in effect*, must be regarded as such, also considering that the transmission mechanism is often contagious. Not unusually, it coincides with increased numbers of alcohol or substance abuse, triggered as an effort to self-medicate. The symptoms are the same as for individual depressions; displaying signs of inadequacy, despondency, lack of vitality, pessimism, sadness and dependency upon substances.[85] Traumas can extend and be prolonged into depressions.[86]

In accordance with the *'frustration-aggression theory,'* aggression is viewed as a reaction to frustration, regardless of source and origin,

---

[83]Lake, David A.; Rothchild, Donald. *The Origins and Management of Ethnic Conflict* International Security, Autumn 1996, Vol. 21, No. 2, p. 41-75.

[84]Updegraff J.A., Silver R.C., Holman E.A. *Searching for and finding meaning in collective trauma: results from a national longitudinal study of the 9/11 terrorist attacks* J Pers Soc Psychol. 2008 Sep,95(3), pp. 709-722.

[85]Bostock, William. *Collective and Individual Depression: Is there a causal link? Perspectives.* 2001, 1 January.

[86]Ibid.

something which is considered biologically coded; some view the frustration-aggression mechanism as the primary source for the human capacity for violence, however there is yet no conclusive evidence to support that notion. In a collective setting, the pent-up feeling of frustration can be released by a political leader that through aggressive rhetoric and agitation, with the promise of violence, offers the desired solution.[87]

A society must be labelled psychologically disturbed if the norms and culture have conformed to the degree that they themselves are causes of psychologically detrimental behavior, much to both Freud's and Fromm's points, and hence its population must gradually adjust to these disturbing patterns not to be considered social (and political) outcasts. And in authoritarian societies, any deviations and digressions from the prescribed norms with its ulterior motives coming down to absolute loyalty, the government typically insists that any deviation would constitute social insanity, with political dissidents occasionally being declared mentally insane.[88]

Collective delusions include the dogmatic belief in political, or religious, slogans and platitudes that once upon a time might have had some validity, but over time have become so detached from reality that continuing to parrot these whilst raising blinders towards deviating perceptions can only be viewed as a delusional exercise. They can be

---

[87]Gurr, Ted R. *Why men rebel* (Princeton, NJ: Princeton University Press, 1970).

[88]Bostock, William. *Collective and Individual Depression: Is there a causal link?* Perspectives. 2001, 1 January.

formulated as false beliefs which are firmly held, despite incontrovertible and obvious evidence to the contrary that no one ordinarily would accept through sober reflection.

Another group mental disorder is collective psychosis, this however differs from other conditions by some distinguishing features as it is a severely disruptive condition that triggers withdrawal in which the distinction between reality and fantasy becomes blurred and may include a return to primitive behavioral patterns.[89] The behaviors meet the criteria for mental disorders, as defined by the DSM-IV-TR; *"disruption in usually integrated functions of consciousness, memory, identity, or perception of the environment and impairment in social, occupational, or other important areas of functioning."*[90]

The Forming Mechanisms of Collectives:
Normal and Norms

What is normal is a truly ambiguous notion and as it is so dynamic, it will vary depending on setting and as difficult such a fluid concept is to pin down, it is still pivotal to understand as individuals and the collective behavior will be regulated by it, whether codified into formal legislation or not, because it becomes such a major influence on how we conduct ourselves. What is normal often only becomes obvious when something *abnormal* occurs, the contrast mainstream-extreme is some-

---

[89]Hinsie, L.E. & Campbell, R.J. *Psychiatric dictionary* (London: Oxford University Press, 4th edition. 1973).

[90]*Diagnostic and Statistical Manual of Mental Disorders*, 4th Edition (2000).

times used in political science. Abnormality is sometimes linked to psychological ailments and the descriptions thereof are or can be used as attempts to define what is outside the boundaries of normality, broadly assuming everything else as normal.[91]

The confines of normal is often, but not always, defined through *norms*; these include values, customs, and traditions to which a collective subscribes. Norms can be arranged as laws, but more often they develop informally as routines to control behavior for some reason deemed harmful.[92] In academia, there have been attempts to formulate the concept of normal; among others, the French sociologist Émile Durkheim (1858-1917) proposed that recurring behaviors among the majority of the population, which he labelled *social facts*, would represent normal, including activities not generally acceptable, such as crime, could also be considered part of what is normal. Even if the criminal behavior of an individual might be perceived as abnormal or unacceptable, on the collective level it averages out and becomes part of the everyday occurrences. Hence, when attempting to forecast human behavior, a distinction needs to be made between the individual and the collective. Such divergence between the individual's normal and the society's normal can manifest in *pluralistic ignorance*, whereby people pay lip service to

[91]Wesley, SP; Nola, JM; Cialdini, RB; Goldstein, NJ; Griskevicius, V. *The constructive, destructive, and reconstructive power of social norms* May 2007. *Psychological Science* 18 (5): 429-434. http://assets.csom.umn.edu/assets/118375.pdf (accessed January 1, 2019).

[92]Bicchieri, C. *The Grammar of Society: The Nature and Dynamics of Social Norms* (New York: Cambridge University Press, 2006) Chapter 1.

the norms that society wants its citizens to adhere to but that they privately abhor. If the contradiction between the privately held norms and the societal ones becomes too wide, too harshly enforced, or too prolonged, at the expense of the ones privately held, the risk for cognitive dissonance will increase, this in itself can lead to psychological disturbances in the form of neurosis.[93] One approach to define normal is through assessing the statistical frequency of various events and to study trends over time to determine when the contents of normal change and to ascertain what the new normal is. The normal and norms therefore produce a reality different from the actual reality, *the social reality*. Society will filter out what does not fall within normal and make projections based on the social reality rather than the actual reality. This has implications, among others, on the language that is set to describe reality and often becomes evident in the constant rewriting of historical events in each new time epoch.[94]

The study on how norms are established is a well-researched area, ranging from Durkheim proposing that norms are the statistically normal behavior, whether morally agreeable or not, to, more recently, Cristina Bicchieri's work on strategies on how to introduce norms to elevate

---

[93]Durkheim, E. The Rules of Sociological Method and Selected Texts on Sociology and its Method (New York: Free Press, 2013).

[94]Shaffer, L.S. *Durkheim's aphorism, the justification hypothesis, and the nature of social facts* Sociological Viewpoints Fall Issue 2006: 57-70. https://www.questia.com/library /journal/1P3-1639680671/durkheim-s-aphorism-the-justification-hypothesis (accessed January 1, 2019)

righteous behavior, yet the reason why normal, or the mainstream, changes over time still puzzles academia.[95]

Conformity and Groupthink

What are then the psychological mechanisms that provide the 'glue' to attach the general public to a reigning zeitgeist? Freud spoke eloquently about herding effects, however in a contemporary setting, the reference is conformity as the act of aligning one's attitudes and behavior to that of the group.[96] The reason for conformity is often based on a desire to seek security within the group rather than risk being a social outcast. Norms therefore form within groups that share some sort of commonality, whether of nationality, ethnicity, religion, etc. By seeking conformity, individuals can come to revert to self-deception and force themselves to consent to the prescribed social reality as presented to them through the zeitgeist, in effect, the peer pressure causes *groupthink*.[97]

---

[95]Bicchieri, C. *The Grammar of Society: The Nature and Dynamics of Social Norms* (New York: Cambridge University Press, 2006) Chapter 6.

[96]Cialdini, RB; Goldstein, NJ. *Social influence: Compliance and conformity* Annual Review of Psychology 2004, 55: 591-621. http://www2.psych.ubc.ca/ ~schaller/ Psyc591Readings/ Cialdini Goldstein2004.pdf (accessed January 1, 2019)

[97]Turner, ME; Pratkanis, AR. *Twenty-five years of groupthink theory and research: Lessons from the evaluation of a theory* Organizational Behavior and Human Decision Processes 1998:73: 105-115. http://www.soc.ucsb.edu/faculty/ friedkin/Syllabi/ Soc147/Week5Req1Reading. pdf (accessed January 1, 2019)

This aspiration for harmony comes at a cost, as the curtailed view of reality leads to inadequate decision-making although at the time it is seen as entirely rational at least to the extent to what everyone outspokenly endorses. The stronger the propensity for groupthink is, the harsher the deviators from the conformist views tend to be treated. To assess whether groupthink is in place, the American psychologist Irving Janis (1918-1990) crafted a suite of criteria that would indicate the existence of groupthink in the collective, whether as society, culture, religion or others:

Type I: Overestimations of the group – its power and morality

• Illusions of invulnerability creating excessive optimism and encouraging risk taking.

• Unquestioned belief in the morality of the group, causing members to ignore the consequences of their actions.

Type II: Closed-mindedness

• Rationalizing warnings that might challenge the group's assumptions.

• Stereotyping those who are opposed to the group as weak, evil, biased, spiteful, impotent or stupid.

Type III: Pressures towards uniformity

• Self-censorship of ideas that deviate from the apparent group consensus.

• Illusions of unanimity among group members, silence is viewed as agreement.

• Direct pressure to conform placed on any member who questions the group, couched in terms of 'disloyalty.'

• Mind guards – self-appointed members who shield the group from dissenting information.

Janis also highlighted three antecedent conditions to groupthink:

• High group cohesiveness;

• Deindividuation: group cohesiveness becomes more important than individual freedom of expression;

• Structural faults;

• Insulation of the group;

• Lack of impartial leadership;

• Lack of norms requiring methodological procedures;

• Homogeneity of members' social backgrounds and ideology;

• Situational context;

• Highly stressful external threats;

• Recent failures;

• Excessive difficulties on the decision-making task, and;

• Moral dilemmas.[98]

---

[98]Janis, IL. *Groupthink: Psychological Studies of Policy Decisions and Fiascoes* (Boston, MA: Cengage Learning, 2nd edition, 1982) Chapters 8 and 9.

The level of adherence to these key elements decides the degree to which contrasting or directly conflicting views outside the realms of conformity are allowed by the governing zeitgeist.

Mass Hysteria and Panics

Conflicting sentiments between the prevailing societal norms and values, and the unconscious drives can create mass hysteria and panics of various intensity. *Mass hysteria*[99] is a collective display of hysterical symptoms, such as unmanageable and excessive exhibits of emotions and loss of self-control, due to overwhelming fear often linked to imagined medical problems or diseases. It tends to coincide with periods of social or economic upheaval. The symptoms of mass hysteria, medically referred to as *mass psychogenic illness*[100] have been extensively studied and psychological stress seems to be a triggering factor. Common features of a hysteric outbreak include the following:

- Symptoms that have no plausible organic basis;

- Symptoms that are transient and benign;

- Symptoms with rapid onset and recovery;

- Occurrence in a segregated group;

---

[99]Bartholomew, Robert E.; Goode, Erich. *Mass Delusions and Hysterias: Highlights from the Past Millennium* Committee for Skeptical Inquiry 24 (May-June 2000). http://www.csicop.org/si/show/mass_delusions_and_hysterias_highlights_from_the_past_millennium (accessed January 1, 2019).

[100]Mass, Weir E. *Mass Sociogenic Illness* Canadian Medical Association Journal 172 (2005): 36.

- The presence of extraordinary anxiety;

- Symptoms that are spread via sight, sound, or oral communication;

- A spread that moves down the age scale, beginning with older people or those of higher status; and

- A preponderance of female participants.[101]

Hysteria is contagious as it has the capability to spread through non-verbal communication as an automatic and unconscious process, which means that it can also transmit through groups without personal physical contact, such as through e-mail and other social media.[102] This form of contagion has been described as follows:

> *When a receiver perceives the emotional expression of the sender, he will automatically imitate these. Through a feedback process the newly adapted emotions will be translated into feelings replicating those of the sender and thus leading to emotional convergence.*[103]

Mass hysteria can also spread through a sort of social pecking order, in which people compare their emotional reactions to those of people with a high social status and then adjust their emotions to match.[104]

---

[101]Ibid.

[102]Jones, Timothy. *Mass Psychogenic Illness: Role of the Individual Physician* American Family Physician 62 (2000), pp. 2649-2653, 2655–2666.

[103]Hatfield, E.; Cacioppo, J.T.; Rapson, R. L. *Emotional Contagion* Current Directions in Psychological Science 2 (1993): 96-99.

[104]Ibid.

A variant is *moral panic*, which is defined as an increased intensity in negative feelings about issues that are considered to threaten social stability.[105] According to the coiner of the term, the South African sociologist Stanley Cohen (1942-2013), moral panic is triggered when a "condition, episode, person, or group of persons emerges to become defined as a threat to societal values and interests."[106] The person or group accused of threatening the social order is referred to as a *folk devil* (read: scapegoat).[107] The topic of disagreement causing the social disturbance is by definition a social taboo, in other words, something not to be touched upon, publicly at least, and expected to be self-censored. Examples of moral panic include the seventeenth century witch trials, McCarthyism, and anti-Semitic pogroms. Moral panics include a number of explicit attributes:

> *Concern.* There must be a perceived awareness that the behavior of the group or category in question is likely to have a negative impact on society;
>
> *Hostility.* Hostility towards the group in question increases, and they become folk devils. A clear division form between "them" and "us";

---

[105]Schoenewolf, G. *Emotional Contagion: Behavioral Induction in Individuals and Groups* Modern Psychoanalysis 15 (1990), pp. 49-61.

[106]Jones, Marsha; Jones, Emma. *Mass Media (Skills-Based Sociology)* (London: Palgrave Macmillan, 1999).

[107]Cohen, Stanley. *Folk Devils and Moral Panics: Creation of Mods and Rockers* (St. Albans: Paladin, 1973), p. 9.

Consensus. Although the concern does not have to be nation-wide, there must be widespread acceptance that the group in question poses a very real threat to society. It is important at this stage that the "moral entrepreneurs" are vocal and the "folk devils" appear weak and disorganized;

Disproportionality. The action taken is disproportionate to the actual threat posed by the accused group, and;

Volatility. Moral panics are highly volatile and tend to disappear as quickly as they appeared, due to a waning in public interest or news reports, changing to another topic.[108]

Conclusions

A collective does have a psychology of its own, however not through some mysterious collective mind, but due to a number of its members responding similarly to psychological stimuli and this because they have conformed through shared values, norms, and culture. These intangibles form a zeitgeist that are representative for a certain era and geography. Prolonged rigidity and stagnation over time renders the zeitgeist outdated and psychologically harmful. The death drive activates to replace the existing zeitgeist with one better-suited for mental vigor.

---

[108]Ibid.

CHAPTER 4
A REVIEW OF CONFLICT THEORIES

The always intriguing development of prosperous societies decaying into ruin has interested scholars since the earliest days of documented human history in the search for the patterns that precede the collapse. It appears to be an almost universal rule that a nation, empire, or civilization eventually sees its demise, and they do so in accordance with a specific set of rules and time span. The most cited examples are the fall of the Roman Empire, and the French and Russian revolutions. There are, in fact, very few nations that have survived intact over the ages and within their core geography; China and Japan being noted exceptions, but they also have seen extended periods and events of revolutions, political violence and been subject to the occupation of foreign powers.

The fall of an empire is, as a rule, generally caused by domestic rather than external factors, however its weaknesses often invites foreign invaders to conquer, and most theories contain a psychological aspect where a sentiment awakens that rejects the existing order and provokes instability. Some hold that these psychological changes reflect a downgrade in the population's genetic composition, and in such cases, the demise is permanent, a hypothesis backed by the historical fact that empires rarely manage to recover. There are indeed other reasons that lead to downfalls apart from changing demographics; the Soviet Union did not collapse due to a deterioration of the population's genetics, but the political system had psychologically stagnated and was not dynamic enough to allow for the necessary psychological revival, to which one can contrast China's successful transition to a (semi-)market economy carefully crafted by its ruling communist party.

The Fate of Empires and Search for Survival

An apt illustration of how a collapse plays out was described by the English Lieutenant General and author, Sir John Glubb (1897-1986), commonly known as *Glubb Pasha*, who at the end of his career launched a theory on the fate of empires in his 1978 *The Fate of Empires and Search for Survival*. Glubb, having spent most of his career serving the British Empire, had, no doubt, been pondering on its hasty demise, sought out the commonalities in the rise and fall of various empires. As the name alludes, Glubb's model was aimed at empires, although he never fully defined that term, but by drawing out the components into a meta model, and with some modifications, it would be applicable also for individual countries, even cities, and civilizations alike. According to him, the fall of an empire takes its starting point in decadence and frivolity, as a consequence of an extended period of affluence, where a younger generation are enjoying the spoils being acquired under hardship and risk taking by an elder generation. These fortunes are being taken for granted, and the skills required to gather them are being downplayed as crude, even vulgar. What he referred to as the *Age of Decadence* is characterized through:

Defensiveness;

Pessimism;

Materialism;

Frivolity;

An influx of foreigners;

The Welfare State, and;

A weakening of religion.[109]

The extended period of wealth and power creates an unbalanced focus on material values, and a shift from loyalty towards the state to a narcissistic perspective. As Glubb explains, the heroes change over time as do their values, soldiers, builders, pioneers and explorers are admired in the initial stages of the imperial life cycle, but during the last stages of decadence and decline, the focus of idolatry has shifted to athletes, musicians and actors, regardless of how corrupt and morally deprived are the private lives of these celebrities.

With a narcissist focus, paired with a decadent lifestyle, comes the erosion of family values and a rampant sexual immorality, typically measured through excessive divorce numbers. Infanticides, and later in times abortions, are on the increase. Sexual perversions, including homosexuality, become socially acceptable, after the existing puritan lifestyle is being down played and ridiculed. Both irresponsible pleasure-seeking and pessimism increase among the population and their leaders. As people cynically give up looking for solutions to the problems of life and society, they begin dropping out of the system. They then turn

---

[109]Glubb, John Bagot. *The Fate of Empires and Search for Survival* (Edinburgh, United Kingdom: Blackwood, 1978).

to mindless entertainment, to luxuries and sexual depravation, and to alcohol and drug abuse.[110]

On the demographic side, family sizes among the well-to-do are on the decrease, whereas among the lower socio-economic strata, through overtly generous welfare systems, children become the source of income, often enough to provide work-free income to also support the parents. These lax and liberal attitudes allow for often uncontrolled immigration, especially settling in the capital of the empire and major cities, creating a cosmopolitan air, but over time leading to ethnic conflicts, as often these immigrant groups come to have a disproportionally high influence, causing discord.[111]

Revolutionary Theories

Already the ancient Greeks explored the causes of political instability that threatened to erupt into violence and shake the foundations of a state. The Greek philosopher Aristotle (384 BC-322 BC), in his famous work on political philosophy *Politics*, devoted a chapter to the study of revolutions. He suggested that there were two types; one that is a complete change of the constitution and another type that merely modifies the existing constitution. As for the causes, Aristotle proposed that poverty among the population was what produced revolutions.[112]

---

[110]Ibid.

[111]Ibid.

[112]Aristotle. *Politics* (Hackett Publishing Company, 1998) book 5.

Another contemporary Greek philosopher, Plato (about 428 BC-about 348 BC) also arrived at the conclusion that poverty was the main cause of revolutions, whereas economic prosperity led to idleness and decadence.[113]

Far later, the French historian Alexis de Tocqueville (1805-1859), whilst investigating the background to the French Revolution, disagreed with the view of poverty as a cause but rather saw that the discontent with the sitting regime was due to a desire to seek political and social reforms in an outdated feudal system.[114]

Albeit, these were early attempts to theorize and forecast revolutions, revolutionary theory first took a more holistic and comprehensive approach with the American historian Crane Brinton (1898-1968) that clearly outlined steps and escalation points of the revolutionary life cycle that he had identified through a study of the main historical revolutions.[115] From the onset of Brinton's theories, the sequel of revolutionary theories, now counting at its fourth generation with each generation seen as a new take on explaining revolutions and its definition, generally mirror the prevalent academic theories of their times. This generational labelling is of a more recent terminology, coined by one of the

---

[113]Plato. *The Republic* (Hackett Publishing Company, 1992) book 8.

[114]Tocqueville, Alexis de. *The Old Regime and the French Revolution* (Dover Publication, 2010) Chapter 20.

[115]Brinton, Crane. *The Anatomy of Revolution* (Prentice-Hall, 1965) Chapter 9.

leading academics of current times, the American historian, Jack Gold-stone.[116]

The First Generation

Goldstone has labelled the first generation of theories as *'the natural history of revolution.'* The characteristic of this first generation was that it was descriptive rather that explanatory. It highlights a suite of common characteristics of revolutions that themselves define what a revolution is. However, little is said of what the actual causes might be.[117]

In the first generation, Brinton, by studying the phases of the English Revolution, the French Revolution, the American Revolution, and the Russian Revolution, highlighted certain commonalities in how the events unfolded and inferred from that a generic *Anatomy of Revolution*, which also came to be the title of his most famous book. His observations were that preceding a revolution, similar societal conditions were in place and once a revolution had occurred, there were a series of steps that most revolutions tended to follow.[118]

---

[116]Goldstone, Jack A. *"Toward a Fourth Generation of Revolutionary Theory"* Annual Review of Political Science, 2001, Vol. 4, pp. 139-187.

[117]Ibid.

[118]Brinton, Crane. *The Anatomy of Revolution* (Prentice-Hall, 1965) Chapter 9.

Brinton defined a revolution as, "a drastic, sudden substitution of one group in charge of a territorial political entity by another group hitherto not running that government."[119]

The symptoms that tended to precede a revolution typically included:

A discontent among the general population, including all social classes;

A sense of restlessness among the people due to societal restrictions, whether imposed by the government, religion, or economic conditions, deemed unacceptable;

The intellectuals no longer endorse the ideology upon which the state operates nor the regime;

The government seems lacking in responsive to the needs of the people, reforms if any are half-hearted;

The reigning power proves inadequate in drumming up sufficient support from the various vested interests;

The state's finances are in doldrums, heading towards bankruptcy or imposing hefty taxes to try to address the budget deficits, and;

---

[119]Ibid., chapter 1.

Revolutionary outbreaks are typically more due to some sort
of crisis occurring rather than pro-active opposition provoking
it.[120]

Feelings of injustice, regardless if justified or not, and the burden of
a struggling economy are the conditions that make a society ripe for a
revolution. Brinton took note of the importance of a changed psychological mood, describing it as a 'fever.' From his observations, Brinton
pointed out that the typical revolutionary was not the lower-class poor
as perhaps expected, but they tended to come from a cross-section of
the social-economic strata. The revolutionaries "behave in a way we
should not expect such people to behave," suggesting that a change in
the psychological mood had taken place.[121]

Brinton also identified sequential steps in the revolutionary cycle;
the unfolding of a revolution commenced with the fall of the old regime,
overthrown by a moderate new government, which in time is replaced
by a more radical movement with tyrannical tendencies to which eventually comes a counter-reaction. But what he failed to adequately answer was the fact that most countries experience times of political tensions and discontent among its populations, yet revolutions still only
rarely occur. Contemporary with Brinton in the 1930s, was the US experiencing the aftermath of the Great Depression, which bore many of the

---

[120]Ibid., chapter 9.

[121]Ibid., chapter 4.

hallmarks of pre-revolutionary sentiments, yet a revolution did not happen. Why was that? Brinton was never really able to provide a clear answer.[122]

And although his work was highly praised among fellow academics for advancing the revolutionary theory considerably, as there were apparent situations it could not explain, alternative theories were to evolve.

The Second Generation

A second generation of theories evolved during the 1960s and 1970s. With the questions *'why'* and *'when'* in the forefront, the scope was broadened, and whereas first-generation scholars took aim at only the main revolutions, i.e. the four big ones; English, American, French and Russian, the second-generation theorists covered a much larger number of cases studies, labelled as *'political violence.'*[123]

The second generation has been split into three different schools of thought; the *psychological approach,* assuming that a revolution is a response to increasing levels of misery or sense of injustice, also referred to as the frustration-aggression theory. The *systematic approach,* which regarded revolutions as the ultimate form of social change and thus assumed it developed out of various forms of disequilibrium within a social system. And finally, the *political approach,* pivoting conflicts between

---

[122]Goldstone, Jack A. *"Toward a Fourth Generation of Revolutionary Theory"* Annual Review of Political Science, 2001, Vol. 4, pp. 139-187.

[123]Radu Alexandru Cucuta. "Theories of Revolution: The Generational Deadlock" *Challenges of the Knowledge Society,* pp. 1107-1116.

interest groups in society, where revolutions would be seen as one of the possible outcomes in power struggles between contesting groups that sidestepped the prescribed decision-making process and instead turned to violence.[124]

One of the more famous hypotheses of the psychological approach was that of the American sociologist James Davies (1918-2012) which proposed a *J-curve*, indicating that political violence had its roots in the aggregate feeling of relative deprivation due to expected economic improvements which 'suddenly' failed to materialize. Hence, the name J-curve, a prolonged uptrend of economic and social improvement is succeeded by period of sharp reversal which graphically depicts a J. This reversal creates an expectation gap and a heightened level of frustration that carries the risk to evolve into a revolutionary mood and launch political violence. According to Davies, what decides political stability or instability is the nature of the collective mood, however the state of dissatisfaction is relative, i.e. there are no absolute material boundaries for when frustration can set in. If applying the J-curve to an economic growth trend, one should thus be able to quite precisely in time pinpoint when there is an increased risk of an eruption of political violence. Hence, revolutions are likely to occur after a period of good economic times followed by a sudden decline of fortunes irrespectively of absolute levels of wealth.[125]

---

[124]Ibid.

[125]Davies, James C. "Toward a Theory of Revolution" *American Sociological Review*, Vol. 27, No. 1 (Feb 1962), pp. 5-19.

The gist of the second generation's assumed root causes to revolutions is that they are the result of a continuous build-up of social or psychological discontent that eventually give forth. They constitute a two-step process; a change of sorts in the present situation differing from the past and that this newly arisen situation presents an opportunity for a revolution to take place. So, whatever factor that was previously not sufficient to trigger a revolution, now holds that capacity. However, it is not a deterministic assumption, if the reigning regime is astute enough to sense the change in sentiment, they can prevent a revolution from occurring through instituting reforms or by applying repressive measures.

The noted problems with the second-generation theories are in finding objective measurement methodologies to assess levels of psychological discontent or disequilibrium within the social system. At what levels of psychological deprivation does it tip over into collective conflict and violence? There were many questions that remained unanswered; would not all cases of political violence be preceded by some sort of discontent? Does that mean that strictly impulsive or instinctive acts of conflict or violence would constitute triggers for revolutions? For the second-generation theorists, it proved hard to develop an early warning system *a priori*. It also seemed that such public frustration that they considered underpinning revolutions occurred far more frequently than the rare episodes of actual revolutions taking place. They could not really explain why revolutions did not occur in other societies in very similar (psychological) situations as the case studies they pointed to.[126]

---

[126]Goldstone, Jack A. "Toward a Fourth Generation of Revolutionary Theory" *Annual Review of Political Science*, 2001, Vol. 4, pp. 139-187.

The Third Generation

The inadequate answers from second-generation theorists on some key points led to further development of revolutionary theory; a third generation unfolded. The third generation also goes under the name *structuralism* and it saw its main works published in the 1960s-1970s. It was clearly influenced by the reigning left-wing spirit in academic circles of the time and took plenty of cues from Marxist theory. This was particularly highlighted in the assumption that it was the struggle between the differing socio-economic classes which was the cause of social and political unrest, and eventually revolutions. And such conflicts typically happened in societies transcending from an agrarian feudal society to a capitalistic industrial system and that transition would create conflicts between the classes over who would control the ownership of the means of production. The move from a capitalistic society towards a socialistic one would be through revolution. But it was not only Marxist theory that inspired third-generation theorists, the works of De Tocqueville were also deployed. In other words, they put the emphasis on the perceived structures that drive revolutions.[127]

They also broadened the structural concept to include in addition to economic classes, rural agrarian-urban conflicts, power struggles between autonomous elites, and how economic and military competition between states influenced domestic political change.

One of the key figures of the third-generation theorists is the American sociologist Theda Skocpol, and her book, published in 1979, *States*

---

[127]Radu Alexandru Cucuta. "Theories of Revolution: The Generational Deadlock" *Challenges of the Knowledge Society*, 2013, pp. 1107-1116.

and Social Revolutions carries many of the characteristics that defined structural thinking. Skocpol also provided her own definition of revolution: "rapid, basic transformations of society's state and class structures...accompanied and in part carried through by class-based revolts from below." The central tenet of her work is that political crisis arose when the state could not meet external challenges because of internal obstacles between the classes; the revolutions in France, Russia, and China respectively provided a common template.[128]

From these studies, Skocpol inferred that the conflicts had not been controlled by any class (or group), no matter how pivotal their efforts are later described in historical reviews, in particular their own. It is thus not the proactive 'making' that creates the possibility for a revolution, but rather structural forces that create revolutionary situations. She also extended to add a theory of revolutionary outcome; it held links to pre-revolutionary factors and drew conclusions from the revolutions of France, Russia and China, these had led to new state formations with more centralized and consolidated powers in relation to the various range of social classes, including the elites.[129]

The Fourth Generation

But the third generation also had its apparent limits, structures just do not change by themselves, they do require proactive actions and these are underpinned by an apparent change in desires and beliefs. So,

---

[128]Skocpol, Theda. *States and Social Revolutions: A Comparative Analysis of France, Russia and China* (Cambridge University Press, 1979) p. 284 ctd.

[129]Ibid, part II.

there was eventually a need to also include elements such as ideology, identification, and leadership as ingredients in the facilitation of revolutions. Skocpol's definition of revolution had ignored ideologies, ethnicity, and religion as basis for revolutionary mobilization, left aside were also the possibility for conflicts within classes and coalitions between classes.

And as the third-generation theorists were overwhelmingly of a left-wing inclination, they, implicitly at least, concurred with the Marxist view that in a communist country no more revolutions or downfall of governments would ever occur. Then with the collapse of the Soviet Union and the socialist satellite states in Eastern Europe happening, the validity of the third generation and its Marxist basis was severely challenged.[130]

A fourth generation emerged in effect becoming a meshed approach, including aspects such as human agency and culture. The fourth-generation academics, with the American political scientist Jack A. Goldstone at their helm, came up with their own definition of revolution, based on an extensive survey listing hundreds of events being revolutionary in character, and excluding events such as coups, revolts, civil wars, and rebellions that did not aspire for social change, as well as peaceful transitions to democracy, such as in Spain after the death of the authoritarian leader Francisco Franco in 1975:

---

[130]Goldstone, Jack A. "Rethinking Revolutions: Integrating Origins, Processes, and Outcomes" *Comparative Studies in South Asia, Africa, and the Middle East*, 2009, Vol. 29, No. 1, pp. 18-32.

an effort to transform the political institutions and the justifications for political authority in a society, accompanied by formal or informal mass mobilization and noninstitutionalized actions that undermine existing authorities.[131]

Goldstone proposed a model to determine when a revolution is highly likely and it is based on a combination of three conditions:

the state is in crisis;

elites are alienated from the state and in conflict with one another; and

a significant part of the population can be mobilized for protest.[132]

Goldstone highlighted: "When any of these factors is weak or absent, a revolution is unlikely; when all are present and strong, revolution is very likely."[133]

In essence, items such as culture and political ideology only matter whether a revolution will bring about a radically new social and political order but it comes down to the three above conditions as prerequisites whether it is at all likely to take place. Regardless of type of political regime and ideology, if there are signs of state crisis, elite conflict, and

---

[131]Goldstone, Jack A. "Toward a Fourth Generation of Revolutionary Theory" *Annual Review of Political Science*, 2001, Vol. 4, p. 142.

[132]Ibid, p. 147.

[133]Keddie, Nikki R (ed) & Goldstone, Jack A. *Debating Revolutions; Predicting Revolutions: Why We Could (and Should) Have Foreseen the Revolutions of 1989-1991 in the U.S.S.R. and Eastern Europe* (New York: NYU Press, 1995) p. 45.

the possibility of political protests, that is enough to rate the risk for revolution as likely.

Eventually, Goldstone expanded his model to twelve components that constitute the revolutionary process. The list of components is as follows:

1. Elite defection and the formation of opposition

2. Polarization and coalition building

3. Mass mobilization

4. Initial regime change

5. Further polarization

6. Counter-revolution

7. Civil war

8. International war

9. Radical regime change and "terror"

10. Revolutionary moderation

11. Renewed radicalism and "terror"

12. Regime consolidation

The first three stages lead up to the initial regime change, and then the stages 5-9 form another suit of connected events, *in one way or an-*

other, and only when radicalism, counterrevolution, and civil and international wars have ended has the revolution reached a stage of moderation and stability, in all not unlike what was proposed by Brinton.[134]

The upgrade to a new generation of theories seems more often than not to occur after a new suite of revolutionary activity that do not follow the expected pattern of previous occurrences, and hence must be *a posterior* adaptation. To sum up, the revolutionary phenomena is still not well understood, especially its psychological components.

Political Ponerology

Political ponerology is the juxtaposition of psychopathology and political science, in particular focusing on the study of the development of authoritarian regimes and their unfolding. Its main proponent was the Polish psychiatrist Andrzej Łobaczewski (1921-2007) who proposed that all societies from a psychological perspective fluctuate between a happy and an unhappy mood. The happy-unhappy distinction being defined by the level of psychopathology dominating the society, and especially its political power, rather than equating it with economic and cultural prosperity, although indirect correlations exist.[135]

[134]Goldstone, Jack A. "Rethinking Revolutions: Integrating Origins, Processes, and Outcomes" *Comparative Studies in South Asia, Africa, and the Middle East*, 2009, Vol. 29, No. 1, p. 20.

[135]Łobaczewski, Andrzej. *Political Ponerology: A Science on the Nature of Evil Adjusted for Political Purposes* (Grande Prairie: Red Pill Press, 2006).

Łobaczewski coined the term *pathocracy* for governments dominated by psychopathic individuals that show a lack of remorse and em-
pathy, disinhibited and egoistical to the point of narcissism. He no
doubt developed the theory with the then-reigning communist regimes
of Eastern Europe in mind. A pathocracy generally quickly evolves into
a totalitarian political system. According to Łobaczewski, such political
systems could develop in societies that are not psychologically
equipped and mature enough to deal with individuals of an abnormal
psychological make-up. Typically, these societies have embarked on a
path of naivety and simplification, being governed by platitudes and
slogans that have turned into dogma with *Orwellian* doublespeak prevailing. In such an atmosphere, psychopaths find it easier to embark on
careers, as normal psychological reactions, norms and values have been
put out of play, as such they can thrive as their psychological disposi-
tions align well with the abnormal settings. Psychopaths are an integral
part of mankind and Łobaczewski views their characteristics as innate
and for these psychopaths, normal rules and norms that regulate human
behavior do not apply, and thus they blatantly circumvent them. The
pathological individuals in the population start to rise through the
ranks and infiltrate political parties, religious and civic organizations,
and over time gain leadership, eventually perverting the original doc-
trines for their own purposes, using them to manipulate society. This
unfolding, Łobaczewski considered part of the *ponerogenic* process. As
their power accumulates, the sense of normal in society is distorted so
that the behavior of pathological groups becomes the norm and what is
perceived as being common sense is regarded as skewed and unnatural.
To uphold their leadership, they typically deploy censoring of the media and by taking control of the education system they introduce methods such as indoctrination and selection of academic leadership based

on political affiliation, as well as adjusting the curriculum to include mandatory subjects that align with their dogmatic beliefs.

Over time, a political system based on loyalty rather than merit regresses to incompetence and corruption in where inefficient management fritters resources and tax revenues, and eventually, the discrepancy between the lofty political ideals *vis-à-vis* reality becomes so obvious and so hard to floss over with propaganda and platitudes that eventually the regime is forced to acknowledge its own shortcomings. This leads to widespread contempt and dissatisfaction amongst the population, and if it gains momentum the government's legitimacy becomes unsustainable. The regime is often undermined through humor manifested as mockery, sarcasm, and irony, pointing out absurdities and deficiencies in the oppressive political system. Hence, a pattern with predictable characteristics in the rise and fall of a pathocracy can be observed, and it typically coincides with the economic peaks and troughs, however often interacting as incompetent governments themselves tend to cause economic difficulties. The advent of pathocracy often occurs in economically prosperous times where over-optimism, even arrogance, lead to an avoidance of anything considered unpleasant and thus any signs of psychopathology in society are overlooked or ignored and thereby allowed to fester and to gain a foothold. By the principle of *live and let live*, psychopaths are allowed to freely express themselves and any attempts to reign them in under mental healthcare treatment are considered reactionary. In due course, psychopathology becomes an integral part of society and it is no longer perceived as a psychological deviation and as psychopaths emerge at leading positions in society, their characteristics become idealized, even considered heroic and their self-serving, narcissistic, instant demands of satisfaction and empower-ment start to negatively influence the whole societal edifice and the in-stitutions and culture that allowed it to prosper in the first place.[136]

Jungian Perspective on War

Jung argued that the unconscious could be a trigger to wars:

> ...the first World War released the hidden power of evil, just as the war itself was released by the accumulation of unconscious masses.... The second World War was a repetition of the same psychic process but on an infinitely greater scale.[137]

To Jung, the two world wars had their root cause in psychological factors rather than political or economic causes. According to him, war was nothing but an expression of an unconscious process in the collective human mind that came to re-enact itself on the world stage. This unconscious process acts to self-correct psychological imbalances, with war being seen as a necessary evil to allow for re-establishing vital cre-ativity and change.[138]

---

[136]Ibid.

[137]Jung, C. G. *Civilization in Transition* (Vol. 10 of *The Collected Works of C. G. Jung*), trans. R. F. C. Hull, 2nd ed. (Princeton, NJ: Princeton University Press, 1981) par. 253.

[138]Lewin, Nicholas. *Jung on War, Politics and Nazi Germany: Exploring the Theory of Archetypes and the Collective Unconscious* (London, UK: Karnac Books, 1st edition, 2009).

He suggested that when the ideas, typically founded on archetypal myths embedded in the collective unconscious, that form a society's narrative and cultural manifestations had lost their attraction this foreboded a society's collapse, as the narrative that bound people together had weakened, even evaporated.[139] With the fall of one archetypal myth, new tensions and new situations are created which bring about an unconscious response and from the new archetype (ideas) arose fresh psychic energy, however the transition period carried an overwhelming risk for aggression and conflict.[140]

Jung proposed that there were cues that could be identified and ascertained to determine the level of archetypal influence in political movements, namely a noted increase in psychological disruptions:

> *mostly in the form of abnormal over- or under-valuations which provoke misunderstandings, quarrels, fanaticisms and follies of every description…*[141]

To him, the most pernicious effect of these archetypal influences was *'the danger of psychic infection.'* Projections play an important role in this process, but they can only occur where there is a grain of truth in them, which makes the projected accusations difficult to counter. As a

---

[139]von Franz, M-L. *Psyche and Matter* (New York: Random House Incorporated, 1992) p. 124.

[140]Jung, C.G. *The Undiscovered Self* (Vol. 10 of *The Collected Works of C. G. Jung*), trans. R.F.C. Hull, 2nd ed. (London, UK: Routledge, 1991, 1957 reprint) par. 549.

[141]Jung, C.G. *The Psychology of the Unconscious* (Vol. 7 of *The Collected Works of C. G. Jung*), trans. R. F. C. Hull, 2nd ed. (London, UK: Routledge, 1990, 1917/1926/1943 reprint) par. 152.

new archetypal force emerges, whilst it does away with old norms and morality, this comes at the cost of undermining the previous social stability.

Conclusions

The conflict theories provide a common, yet little researched, denominator, namely that the transition from a previous well-to-do society that suddenly becomes marred by discontent likely to erupt into violence is brought about by a change in psychological sentiment. Attempts to forecast the rare events leading to radical societal changes, such as revolutions and wars, have been numerous over the centuries; from the French Revolution and Russian Revolution up to the fall of communism in Eastern Europe and the more recent Arab Spring. It is here that the concept of the death drive fits the bill well, its activation to seek to destroy what is psychologically harmful, which at the collective level means overthrowing a regime through violent means if necessary, or starting a war to undermine a culture or civilization that have become *too* restrictive and stagnant.

CHAPTER 5

WHAT TRIGGERS THE DEATH DRIVE?

An era can be said to end when its basic illusions are exhausted

— Arthur Miller, American essayist (1915-2005)

Conformity of Thought Prompts Mental Stagnation

The death drive carries ultimate healing effects in that it forces what has been repressed and suppressed to emerge at the conscious level, thereby expanding the awareness so that existing taboo issues can be addressed and dealt with in a rational manner. The psychological atmosphere in a society guided by political or religious dogmas that over time no longer align with reality means that there is an ever-increasing number of taboos themes that have fallen outside the norms of acceptable topics and no longer can be openly discussed. It leads to the public debate and general discourse being suffocated and a great psychological shadow comes to exist which the population must conform to through circumvention as they are being caged by the many taboos. The discrepancy between the narrow narrative of 'allowed' topics *vis-à-vis* an unbending and uncompromising reality causes the defense mechanisms to work in overdrive. But the excessive amount of perceptions that are forced to be excluded from the social reality increases the risk of psychological ill-health as it creates an artificial and distorted view of the world that eventually becomes unsustainable and ever more difficult to adhere to.

In a society where the focus is on a certain set of norms that are expected to be shared by its citizens and enforced through various means, including scores of propaganda, this extended collective focus comes at the expense of individual development. Eventually traits of indolent and stagnating patterns are noticed as individual initiatives throughout many aspects of life come with the risk of being perceived as a non-conformist and singled out as an instigator of social disharmony. This causes changes in human behavior as implicit lethargy becomes the easy-out strategy to escape the risk of being accused of not conforming, or being guilty of 'offensive' comments. So, to avoid unpleasant aspects of reality, self-deception, much the way the French philosopher Jean-Paul Sartre (1905-1980) described it, is deployed.[142] And as Freud posited, the fantasies that exist in the psychological reality instead becomes the self-deceiving guiding principles, in a sense providing social blinders and allowing for not having to observe the obvious that is in front of us.[143]

---

[142]Freud, Sigmund. *Formulations on the Two Principles of Mental Functioning* (London: Routledge, first edition, 2016 reprint, 1911) p. 218.

[143]Freud, Sigmund. *Group Psychology and the Analysis of the Ego* (New York: W.W. Norton & Company, Revised edition, 1990 reprint, 1921) p. 80.

As the ego has become weakened through the excessively repressive society, there is a conscious lack of endurance to stand-up against all propaganda being produced, so the platitudes *en vogue* become part of the everyday jargon, being repeated until they are a formative part of the discourse. Thus, there will be little in terms of thoughtful understanding of the dominating ideology as repetitive slogans come to suffice, and, as such, truly open debates are being avoided, or deliberately undermined as the supporters of the reigning dogma rarely can speak up for their views which are merely mired buzz words. It becomes a stark contrast to a society that recognizes and addresses its problems through debate, albeit at times heated. But a dogmatic ideology rarely acknowledges any weaknesses in its creed and works to sustain an ideal view of itself, with problems being covered up, however, this becomes a breeding ground for mental disturbances. And it allows for mentally disturbed people to come to power, much in accordance with the theories of political ponerology, as neurotic and narcissistic conditions inevitably become the reigning norm, even seen as an ideal to adhere to and a lack of self-awareness comes to qualify as a career enhancing characteristic. However, whilst consciously paying lip service to the prescribed slogans, the unconscious is working toward its demise and as the destructive attitudes and actions are viewed as liberating in that rests a joy in the destruction.[144]

Jung could provide historical examples of stagnation, arguing that the period of Enlightenment through its feudal system had stagnated and it refused to reform itself and thus ended with the horrors of the

---

[144]Jung, C.G. *Collected Works of C.G. Jung*, Volume 7: *Two Essays in Analytical Psychology* (New Jersey: Princeton University Press, 1967).

French Revolution as a marker for destruction and renewal. He also drew parallels with what was happening in the then contemporary Europe of the 1930s with both communism and fascism on the rise as a protest to stagnating societal systems and prophesized that, like the French Revolution, it would end in mass-murder on an unparalleled scale. To Jung, it highlighted the objective of the unconscious and these emerging mass movements were defined by elements of irrationalism, even resorting to mysticism, which explained why their popularity becomes so difficult to understand through the instruments of political science which operate solely on rational analysis.[145]

But as Jung did not subscribe to the death drive concept, he rather viewed it as a release of psychic energy, *mana*, being charged into a new archetype, and with that new thought patterns being constellated, as such replacing a previously reigning archetype which becomes obsolete as it is no longer meaningfully can relate to reality. The shift between archetypes causes psychological disturbances in society, and according to him one could search for the theme of the new archetype that forms the emerging zeitgeist in the previous taboo areas. In his essay *Wotan* from 1936, Jung described the activation of the archetype Wotan in Germany and how that had facilitated a psychological environment that promoted national socialism. He explained how certain individuals (read: Adolf Hitler) could be so encapsulated by such psychological atmosphere that they came to act as figureheads for the affiliated movements, whether it be of a political-, cultural- or religious nature, that represented and harmonized with the looming archetype. He described Hitler as an empty shell that had been loaded and energized by mana,

---

[145]Ibid.

which explained Hitler's quality as a demagogue as he through it could appeal to Germany's collective unconscious. So, Jung argued that a rational analysis of Hitler was bound to be misleading, but that he instead must be examined from a psychological perspective, and described him as a sort of *shaman*. These shaman types need not fully understand the nature of their forceful psychological influence and the mechanics that lead to that seemingly unexplained popularity, but that they at least have the presence of mind to use it to their full advantage.[146]

One need however to differentiate between the changes forced through by the death drive and the changes of a dynamic culture that adapts to new circumstances. This as change is not endemic in all cultures, as some come to fall into patterns of stagnancy and sterility with profoundly low levels of awareness of the world that surrounds it, and constantly falling back on ignorant and naïve perspective. This can be due to that culture being high-jacked by an intolerant leadership that only through rebellious means can be returned to its previously vibrant nature, or the culture itself is stagnant as it corresponds to its population's cognitive constraints, satisfying itself with mundane explanations of reality and aligning the society and norms accordingly. In contrast, a truly dynamic culture facilitates and incorporates changes, as reality through technological, political, or some other exogenous factors continuously evolve.

The subscription by the *hoi polloi* to various political ideologies and religious affiliations that are endorsed by the death drive must thus be understood psychologically rather than from the perspective of political

---

[146]Jung, C. G. *Collected Works of C.G. Jung,* Volume 10: *Civilization and Transition, Wotan.* (London: Routledge and Kegan Paul, 1970) p. 185.

or religious convictions. And by affiliating oneself to such movements comes the possibility to actively engage in destructive and castigating activities which define the very nature of the death drive, and more often than not it is conducted with great lust as it brings with it psychological renewal. Therefore, the features of these political/religious movements share psychological commonalities regardless of time epoch and geography, so an individual influenced by the psychology of a current death drive would, in the political settings of the 1930s, undoubtedly have found himself at home in either communist or fascist movements as representing the disruptive forces of the time. As such, it is never really about certain political or religious inclinations but a motivational process of undermining and destroying the circumstances that hinders psychological fulfilment. This explains why such movements tend to fall back on banal and unsophisticated slogans, as an in-depth understanding of the issues at hand is absent and there is intellectually no need for it, as destruction is the psychological pivot.

In cultures with a deficiency of true individualism, and where an absent capacity for independent thinking and creative ability are notable features, it creates a society which is lacking in awareness, as it is reverting to collective identity and group think, in essence, forcing man to become alienated from his own distinctive character. For the collective ideology only seeks out the common man where no distinctions are allowed to exist, such as the *Lysenkoistic* attempts in the Soviet Union with the extermination of class enemies, or Nazi attempts to form an Aryan race and waging war on scapegoated races. In effect, a dehumanization process also takes place within the preferred group, each replaceable by another like pieces of *Lego*, and any outsiders will eventually come to cease to exist as human subjects, so that in the end only the stereotype remains. A heavy-handed, castigating approach, including violence, against groups marked as scapegoats becomes an inevitable part of the process, the degree depending on the fervor of the death drive. As awareness levels have been so reduced, anything marked as unknown, foreign, etc., comes to prompt great anxiety as the collectively reduced human consciousness struggles to relate to it and the aggressive behavior provides some momentarily relief and feeling of empowerment.

The obsession with destruction creates an *us and them* perspective, constantly seeking scapegoats to blame, and anything considered impure must be eradicated as it stands in the way to the establishment of a worker's paradise, caliphate, thousand-year Reich, or similar utopic visions. The demand for political or religious cleanliness is enhanced by the authorities' efforts to ban words deemed forbidden, introducing euphemisms, in effect trying to outlaw illegal thoughts and introducing dogmatic unquestionable truths. In the end, everything that resembles independent individual thinking must cease. But with the lack of critical thinking, the human collective regresses to infantilism and hibernation as anything that confronts the prescribed worldview and appears problematic must be silenced and brushed under the carpet.

Behavioral Changes

As the repressive society considers evermore topics taboo, in order to uphold the pretext of normality in such an unbalanced environment, *delusions* serve as a fitting behavioral mechanism where they are allowed to form an extreme interpretation of reality to ensure the adherence to the dogmatic beliefs. Delusion is a psychiatric term highlighting the manifestations of erroneous ideas about reality, either about oneself or the external world, which by the objective bystander is considered not to be true, in essence the delusional ideas are regarded as absurd.[147] *Folie à deux* is the term used to describe collective delusions, typically categorized as mass psychosis or conspiracy theories. What characterizes delusions is that they are expressed with an unusual conviction to the point that any disagreeing evidence will rarely convince one of the conviction's falseness.[148] They come to play a defining part in the life of the individual or collective with humor and irony generally frowned upon, even met with aggression, in particular when the delusional ideas are being challenged.[149]

Delusions occur as part of a pathological state but need not to be affiliated with any particular psychological illness, however it can appear in schizophrenia, manic stages, and psychotic depression. The traditional definition of delusion consists of three criteria established by the German-Swiss psychiatrist and philosopher Karl Jaspers (1883-1969) in his 1913 book *General Psychopathology*. These criteria are:

certainty, ideas held with absolute conviction;

-----

[147]The ICD-10 Classification of Mental and Behavioural Disorders, Clinical descriptions and diagnostic guidelines http://www.who.int/classifications/icd/en/bluebook.pdf

[148]Jaspers, Karl. *General Psychopathology*, volumes 1 & 2 translated by J. Hoenig and Marian W. Hamilton. (Baltimore and London: Johns Hopkins University Press. 1997).

[149]Yamada N, Nakajima S, Noguchi T. "Age at onset of delusional disorder is dependent on the delusional theme." *Acta Psychiatrica Scandinavica*. 97 (2). February 1998. pp. 122-124.

incorrigibility. not changeable by compelling counterargument or proof to the contrary, and;

impossibility or falsity of content, the ideas are simply implausible, bizarre, or patently untrue.[150]

Self-deception is a somewhat less severe form of refusing to view reality objectively compared to delusion. Freud claimed that neurotics deceived themselves "because they find it (*author's note*: reality) unbearable – either the whole or parts of it."[151]

Thus, delusions and self-deceptions become common features in the psychological environment that defines a stagnating worldview. To Freud, it represented an unfilled wish as part of neurosis:

> *We have found that what neurotics are guided by is not ordinary objective reality but psychological reality.*[152]

Liminality

Liminality is the phase where a shift between zeitgeists is ongoing, hence it is defined as a *temporary* condition, a no-man's land of sorts, where there is a limbo in what norms or culture one should adhere to.

---

[150]Jaspers, Karl. *General Psychopathology – Volumes 1 & 2* translated by J. Hoenig and Marian W. Hamilton. (Baltimore and London: Johns Hopkins University Press. 1997).

[151]Freud, Sigmund. *Formulations on the Two Principles of Mental Functioning* (London: Routledge, first edition, 2016 reprint, 1911) p. 218.

[152]Freud, Sigmund. *Group Psychology and the Analysis of the Ego* (New York: W.W. Norton & Company, Revised edition, 1990 reprint, 1921) p. 80.

One is in effect between sets of culture and ambiguity holds sway, as the new cultural order has yet to be established and compliance with the old one is waning. It is a threshold moment.[153]

This moment of ambiguity leads to individual identities being disoriented as they are flushed through a vortex of old and new perspectives and it is usually marked as psychologically intense. This phase of disorientation and dissolution creates a dynamic and fluid situation which allows for new norms and institutions to be formed and eventually, *liminality* comes to an end as the new cultural format becomes generally endorsed.[154]

The three phases of *liminality* are structured as:

Moment; occurs as the society faces an event, typically of an exogenous nature such as an invasion, epidemic or natural disaster, or a revolution, that causes collapse of social order;

It is followed by *Period*; characterized by violent conflict, and finally;

---

[153]Szakolczai, Arpad. "Liminality and Experience: Structuring transitory situations and transformative events" (*International Political Anthropology*, 2 (1), 2009) p. 141.

[154]Ibid.

Epoch; a stage with continued political instability and confusion on which a new set of culture and norms come to dominate, embedded through drawing on incorporation and repro-
duction as forming structures.[155]

The age of *liminality* is also highlighted by spurts of creativity,
where radical ideas are allowed to flounder being incentivized by the
uncertainties that affects entire civilizations and unhindered by previous conventions. It is hence a time of both destruction and construction
with some of the ideas being formed having lasting values for the coming era. However, it is also a phase of unknown and unpredictable outcomes, as it is generally not guided by any 'invisible hand' and as such
it contains a distinct possibility of erupting into conflict.[156]

Subversive Affirmation

The first protests against a repressive political climate often start
through *subversive affirmation*, where artists in their creative expressions
over-exaggerate the ideological elements and manifestations to the
point that they might from certain perspectives be regarded as ridicu-
lous in their apparent overzealous devotions. At first, the dissents are
driven by unconscious forces, however, over time, the sentiments are
no longer psychologically submerged but enter the artist's awareness
from where on the over-exaggerated expressions are done deliberately
as a satirical critique against the regime. The subversive element is at

---

[155]Thomassen, B. "The Uses and Meanings of Liminality" (*International Political
Anthropology*, 2 (1). 2009) p. 19.

[156]Ibid.

times so subtle that it is only subliminally recognized and it is essentially the surplus information in the artistic pieces that form the subversive element. Whilst with explicit enthusiasm honoring the political message, the overemphasis on certain aspects comes *de facto* to undermine the ideological tenets. This type of over-identification tends to be a more frequent feature towards the end phase of repressive regimes. It was a prevalent method in the Communist era in Eastern Europe as a way to protest against the Soviet-style political dictatorship and it reached its peak in the 1960s and 1970s preluding the *Prague Spring* in 1968 and the 1980s *Solidarność* movement in Poland.[157]

Cultural Manifestations – Decadence and Degeneration

As previously detailed, Glubb Pasha wrote about decadence as a pre-cursor towards the collapse of empires and argued that it eventually would affect all affluent societies, manifesting as the values necessary for accumulation of wealth and its required attitudes, such as industriousness and pioneering, being replaced by leisurely endeavors requiring little risk taking or hard work. Heroism succeeded by hedonism, going so far that eventually heroism is being ridiculed.

Max Nordau (1849-1923), the Austro-Hungarian Jewish author and social critic commented on the degeneration that he saw as a prominent feature among his contemporaries in one of his most famous books *Degeneration* (*Entartung*) from 1892. Nordau theorized that continental Europe influenced by *fin de siècle* and that the affluence created from the

[157]Arns, Inke; Sasse, Sylvia. *Subversive Affirmation. On Mimesis as Strategy of Resistance* Editorial, spring 2006 issue of Maska, Ljubljana.

ongoing industrialism and urbanization had led to the degeneration of cultural elites to varying degrees, and as such suffering mentally. He defined them as:

> That which nearly all degenerates lack is the sense of morality and of right and wrong... when this phenomenon is present in a high degree, we speak of "moral insanity"... there are, nevertheless, lower stages in which the degenerate does not, perhaps, himself commit any act which will bring him into conflict with the criminal code, but at least asserts the theoretical legitimacy of crime; seeks, with philosophically sounding fustian, to prove that "good" and "evil," virtue and vice, are arbitrary distinctions; goes into raptures over evildoers and their deeds; professes to discover beauties in the lowest and most repulsive things; and tries to awaken interest in, and so-called "comprehension" of every bestiality.[158]

As civilizations over time advance, in particular economically, they come at risk of degenerating with hereditary consequences and signs of it could be studied from the emerging art movements. Nordau noted an almost obsessive interest for abnormalities, the bizarre and perversities, including stories about serial killers, serving as a defining characteristic of a degenerate culture, and typically to pique the interest among the general populace, art works increasingly covered these themes. His claim that pathology, including sadistic crimes, coincides with mental disturbances, is a hypothesis that has been verified in later studies, high-

---

[158]Nordau, Max. *Degeneration* (Nebraska: University of Nebraska Press; Reprinted edition 1993 translated, 1892).

lighting that individuals showing psychotic traits often write about various aspects of pornography, butchers, decapitations and other morbid features.[159]

Nordau was skeptical that degenerates and the societies they formed could survive over an extended period as they would eventually become too detached from reality:

> *Degenerates, hysterics and neurasthenics are not capable of adaptation. Therefore, they are fated to disappear. That which inexorably destroys them is that they are not able to come to terms with reality. They are lost, whether they are alone in the world, or whether there are people with them who are still sane. They live, like parasites, on labour which past generations have accumulated for them; and when the heritage is once consumed they are condemned to die of hunger.[160]*

Some animal experiments have highlighted the mechanisms that cause degenerate societies. Through studies on rats and mice conducted by the American ethologist John B. Calhoun (1917-1995), he developed the concept of *behavioral sink*. Whilst the studies analyzed the situation of rodent overpopulation, parallels can be drawn to welfare societies in where the population got more or less unlimited access to food, water and entertainment. In the experiments, the rodents were not required to 'work', i.e. to find food, hence no longer needed to struggle to survive but could mate, recreate, and eat in excess, in a sense creating a utopia.

---

[159]Pick, Daniel. *Faces of Degeneration. A European disorder, c.1848-c.1918* (Cambridge, UK: Cambridge University Press, 1989).

[160]Nordau, Max. *Degeneration* (Nebraska: University of Nebraska Press; Reprinted edition 1993 translated, 1892).

However, the paradise situation was not to last as a behavioral sink situation developed, the indolence led to the female mice stopped caring for its offspring, leaving them in neglect. The male mice no longer wanted to mate, but turned to aggression, cannibalism, and homosexual behavior. Another group of male mice stopped interacting altogether, showing no interest in mating and no signs of aggressive behavior, becoming outright lethargic and passive. All they did was eat, sleep, and groom themselves. Eventually the population died out as so few were interested in mating and the continuous infighting leading to a large number killing off each other. The outcome was mainly due to overpopulation that the free access to food and shelter had created, but at the same time, elements of degenerate behavior provoked a type of rodent death drive.[161]

The English ethologist J.D. Unwin (1895-1936), in his *Sex and Culture* from 1934 studied 80 tribes and 6 known civilizations over 5,000 years of history and found a positive correlation between cultural achievement and the level of sexual restraint observed.[162] According to Unwin, the growing prosperity of a country triggers an increasingly liberal sexual morality and over time it starts to lose its economic and cultural vitality and purpose to prosper, a process which he claimed was irreversible:

---

[161]Calhoun, John B. "*The Social Aspects of Population Dynamics*" (Journal of Mammalogy. American Society of Mammalogists. 33 (2), 1952) pp. 139-159.

[162]Unwin, Joseph Daniel. *Sex and Culture* (London: Oxford University Press, 1934).

The whole of human history does not contain a single instance of a group becoming civilized unless it has been absolutely monogamous, nor is there any example of a group retaining its culture after it has adopted less rigorous customs.[163]

Unwin shared the Freudian view that civilization progressed as a product of instinctual constraints, with sexual ones playing a key role, by directing the finite human energy (or libido in Freudian terms) towards industrious risk ventures instead of sexual adventures. Unwin explained that mankind possessed two categories of collective energy, an *expansive* and a *productive*. Expansive energies are focused towards commerce, conquest and territorial expansions. Productive energies are targeted toward the advancement of society through innovation. Unwin argued that to ensure prosperity sexual energy should be directed toward any of these instead. He remarked:

The evidence is that in the past a class has risen to a position of polit-ical dominance because of its great energy and that at the period of its rising, its sexual regulations have always been strict. It has retained its energy and dominated the society so long as its sexual regulations have demanded both pre-nuptial and post-nuptial continence. ... I know of no exceptions to these rules.[164]

In his view, the ideal society was based on heterosexual monogamy as that provided the optimal arrangement for planning, establishing, protecting, and nurturing families, which was what formed the nucleus

---

[163]Unwin, Joseph Daniel. *"Monogamy as a Condition of Social Energy"* (The Hibbert Journal, Vol. XXV, 1927) p. 662.

[164]Ibid.

that provided the stable social edifice upon which an economy could prosper. But with growing affluence came work-free income through inheritance, rentiers, etc., which carried the peril of prompting an increase in promiscuity that drew energy from innovation and further economic development as the pressure to work for one's survival no longer remained. This liminality phase with changing norms and preferences toward unbalanced economic windfalls and contributions drew the risk of creating an economically and socially decisive society which held the propensity to end in violent conflicts.

The terms decadence and degeneration are completely gone from the vocabulary in today's cultural and political discourse, however it used to carry great significance in previous debates, not only applied by conservatives, but also playing an important role in Marxist analysis, for them, however, it was more focused on economic factors rather than spiritual voids and loose morals due to extended periods of exuberant prosperity. The terms have sometimes been used interchangeably however they differ in meaning as decadence signifies cultural and moral decline, and degeneration a decline from normality into abnormal standards not seldom due to a genetic impoverishment through undesirable immigration or high birth rates among less developed cognitive groups. Thus, decadence often coincides with prosperous groups' switch from an industrious and entrepreneurial lifestyle towards hedonism and debauchery, something which Marxists often attacked. Degeneration, however, came to be more closely linked with the eugenics movement and their concern about a permanently deteriorating quality of the population.

Artistic Manifestations – Grotesque, Bizarre, and Perverse

The timing of the concerns of a degenerating society was not coincidental as Europe and North America saw unprecedented economic growth and scientific development in the last decades of the nineteenth century and the first of the twentieth century, and the riches allowed for exploring new paths in art and culture, some drastically breaking with previous views of aesthetic symmetry as the standard definition of beauty in all forms of art including literature, painting, and music. The decadent art movement of the late nineteenth century came to renounce the harmonious requirements, instead distorting symmetry in perspectives and proportions, and color arrangements by proactively seeking disharmony. Many of its themes had the characteristics of being freakish, often just to stir up attention and curiosity, and perversions in its many aspects came to play a noted part. In literature, stories about freaks and monsters became bestsellers, including *The Strange Case of Dr. Jekyll and Mr. Hyde* from 1886 by the Scottish author Robert Louis Stevenson (1850-1894) and the Irish author Abraham 'Bram' Stoker's (1847-1912) *Dracula* from 1897. The genre was labelled *Gothic Horror*.[165, 166]

Of course, a cultural fad cannot hold sway unless there is genuine public demand for it. *Fin de siècle* neo-romanticism came to represent the

---

[165]Heffernan, Michael. "The Politics of the Map in the Early Twentieth Century" (*Cartography and Geographic Information Science*, 29/3, 2002). p. 207.

[166]Maxwell, Catherine. "Theodore Watts-Dunton's 'Aylwin (1898)' and the Reduplications of Romanticism" (*The Yearbook of English Studies*, 37.1. 2007). pp. 1-21.

gist of the various art streams at the end of the nineteenth century extending up to World War I, typically dealing with anxiety, feeble nerves, a general fatigue of life, and decadence, as well as the aforementioned horrors and perversions. It was often expressed through symbolism with mysticism and obscurity replacing the previous guiding stars of clarity, logic, and precision, and with the sublime distinguishing between the apparent and abstract. Art serving utilitarian purposes, such as being objects of (eternal) beauty and inspiring to elevate human aspirations were no longer a priority, even when it was produced to promote a political message. Instead, art aimed to free people from morals and rationality with a focus on spirit and soul. This revolt against materialism and rationalism, and the attacks on the burgeoning democracy to the benefit of emotionalism and irrationalism, has later been accused of providing a fertile breeding ground for fascism that sought to overhaul the decadent bourgeoisie society, something that would gain power-shifting popularity a few decades later.[167]

Neurosis - Cultural Diseases

Neurosis is a collective term for various psychological conditions, including anxiety, hysteria, distress, phobias, and obsessive disorders. It typically manifests as anger, irritability, sadness or depression, but also as compulsive acts and inappropriate behavior. As it covers so many symptoms, it has been hard to systematically it track over time

---

[167]Zeev, Sternhell. "Crisis of Fin-de-siècle Thought" (*International Fascism: Theories, Causes and the New Consensus.* London and New York, 1998) p. 169.

and between cultures.[168] Neurosis should not be mistaken for neuroticism which is a fundamental personality trait manifested in moody and nervous behavior, whilst neurosis is a distortion of reality, albeit the terms are often used interchangeably. The root causes to neurosis are generally considered diffuse and society are often ill equipped to provide adequate treatments, and with the lack of effective remedies, it tends to linger on usually fading away over time transcending to another syndrome with similar symptoms.

From the Freudian perspective, neurosis is seen as a binding condition simply by partaking in civilization, difficult therefore to avoid. The upholding of a normalcy by denying some instinctual needs comes to incorporate neurosis as an integral part of society. More specifically, it is through the defense mechanisms that neurosis is provoked, producing a distorted way of looking at the world and at oneself, determined by restraints rather than by a genuine human way of accepting reality as it is. But as it results in anxiety and distress, it is therefore not a desirable compromise between society's culture and human instincts. Hence, there are hypocritical aspects of societal life that stand as the root cause to neurosis.

To Freud and his contemporaries, the particular type of neurosis was hysteria, or *neurasteni*, prevalent in the European culture, in particularly affecting women in the constrained social and cultural environment that defined the Victorian era. Hysteria encapsulated and channeled a whole generation of women's fatigue, anxiety and depressive

---

[168]Boeree, George. C. *A Bio-Social Theory of Neurosis 2002.* http://webspace.ship.edu/cgboer/genpsyneurosis.html

mode as society repressed many of their natural urges, notably sexuality, into the unconscious.

In more recent years, The American Diagnostic and Statistical Manual of Mental Disorders (DSM) have eliminated the category of neurosis from its list of psychological disorders. This due to a move away from hidden psychological mechanisms as diagnostic criteria towards the description of behaviors, therefore the previous label neurosis will today appear as various anxiety disorders and often fall under the collective term *cultural disease*.[169, 170]

A cultural disease is defined according to the following criteria:

Is being viewed as a disease exclusively occurring in a certain era and context and is being labelled and spread within a defined culture with its norms, narratives and threats;

Most of its symptoms are of a diffuse character and cannot be biologically verified, and;

It vanishes over time as it is no longer regarded as a disease by the medical expertise, or another cultural disease replaces it due to changing circumstances.[171]

---

[169]Horney, Karen. *Neurosis and Human Growth: The Struggle Toward Self-Realization* (W.W. Norton & Company, Inc. 1950). p. 18.

[170]Bailey, Hamilton. *Demonstrations of physical signs in clinical surgery* (First ed.). Bristol: J. Wright and Sons, 1927) p. 208.

[171]Johannisson, Karin. "Om begreppet kultursjukdom" (*Läkartidningen* nr. 44 2008 volym 105) pp. 3129-3132.

Hence, a cultural disease carries obscure characteristics in a specific cultural context and the symptoms are adjusted to fit society's sanctioned paradigms. For a cultural disease to become 'successful' it must reflect the contemporary threats the society is exposed to or at least what it perceives to be a threat, with the symptoms of stress and anxiety being distinguished and defined as a sanctioned outlet and coping mechanism. At the root of the cultural disease is a preference for the subjective illusion ahead of reality, and when aspects of reality have diverged too far away from the preferred illusion, it prompts the condition:

> *Only psychic realities and not actual ones are at the basis of the neurotics,' sense of guilt. It is characteristic of the neurosis to put a psychic reality above an actual one and to react as seriously to thoughts as the normal per son reacts only towards realities.*[172]

As society evolves and with it the threats it is exposed to, the cultural disease changes with it, however the symptoms remain remarkably similar. Often these arise around themes characterized as taboos, boosted as people, afraid of conflict, at length try to seek out conformity, so inhibited aggression becomes a key factor where to look for areas which the cultural disease can be affiliated with. Thus, a politically or religiously stagnating society with its demand for conformity, the many taboo areas, and the sweeping of problems under the carpet, provide an environment that is prone to develop cultural diseases, sometimes these can be labelled and quite clearly defined, however with its symptoms carrying such vague properties, the malaise is at times classified as a

---

[172]Freud, Sigmund. *Totem and Taboo: Resemblances Between the Mental Lives of Savages and Neurotics* (New York: W.W. Norton & Company; The Standard Edition, 1990, translated, 1913). p. 185.

general fatigue or a type of depression which are not always clearly distinguished.

Cultural epidemiology is a term minted by the American anthropologist James A. Trostle in his 2005 book *Epidemiology and culture*, where he studied the contagion mechanism of cultural diseases, explained through a convergence process. He found that many of these cultural diseases first emerged among groups that demonstrated particular mobility with regards to socio-economics. Amongst the first noted to suffer from a cultural disease at the turn of the last century were members of the burgeoning *bourgeoisie*, such as merchants, high-ranking bureaucrats, academics, and scientists, and contemporary medical records confirm a large number of males from the upper classes as being diagnosed at the outbreak stage. But as hysteria started to spread amongst the population, gaining traction in other groups and becoming more frequent amongst women and the lower classes, it lost its 'prestige' and the number of upper-class men being diagnosed correspondingly dropped notably. Trostle regarded these cultural diseases as a socially acceptable outlet to deal with problems that a society is not geared to meet, this as aspects of reality for various reasons are constraining pragmatic remedies. A cultural disease therefore comes to function as a form of acceptable protest, or refuge, by a society that is unable to address and to solve enduring problems and gives it consent for it, at least implicitly, as the alternative could be rioting and political violence. Thus, authorities grant an approved medical diagnosis through 'sympathetic' medical professionals, and the patients have been given a *'carte blanche'* to excuse himself to his employer, colleagues, family, and friends, allowing for the status quo of the society to be maintained and upheld. So, each time epoch tends to have its own cultural diseases. How widespread these diseases are depends upon the gravity of the underlying problem, but they are serving the same purpose; to meet the need of being able to control a world one does not fully comprehend and by accepting it as safety valve to escape to, it in a sense becomes source of comfort as the patients now can identify and legitimize their behaviors with the cultural disease.[173, 174]

The feelings of anxiety and distress are the defined commonalities, however nowadays more indefinite symptoms of general pain, psychosomatic syndromes and functional disturbances have additionally come to define a cultural disease. Also, currently cultural diseases rarely carry their previous prestige, instead they are generally viewed as low status and the medical profession struggles with remedies and rehabilitation, often turning to low doses of various types of narcotics to alleviate the symptoms, notably ADHD (attention deficit hyperactivity disorder) falls into that category. It is now considered that the cultural diseases express some sort of crisis and an inability to cope in societies' various forums. The term *civilization syndrome* has been introduced to provide a broader description of the condition.[175]

Cultural diseases tend to prevail and accelerate in numbers during times of great change, including increased flow of information and com-

---

[173]Trostle, James A. *Epidemiology and Culture* (Cambridge Studies in Medical Anthropology) (Cambridge: Cambridge University Press, 2005).

[174]Johannisson, Karin. *Den mörka kontinenten: kvinnan, medicinen och fin-de-siècle* (Stockholm, Sweden: Nordstedts Förlag, 1994).

[175]Björtorp, P., Holm, G., & Rosmond, R. "Neuroendokrina störningar ger stressrelaterad sjukdom. 'Civilisationssyndromet' ett växande hälsoproblem" (*Läkartidningen*, 99, 1999), pp. 893-896.

munications, and new (and increased) professional demands on workers, in all cases the individual man feels reduced to a small cog in the
economic wheel, easily replaceable by another, with his value equaling
his economic contributions and little else. It is in such an environment
that mankind struggles to psychologically cope, and it takes its toll in
increasing numbers of mental discomforts and ailments. In other words,
it is a culture where strong competition, performance, and stress levels
are decisive for success, and an accelerating pace of change plays a more
important role than what was previously perceived to have been the
case. Feelings of restlessness, dissatisfaction, not being on top of things,
both physically and psychologically, and a sense of being insufficient
and not really mattering in the grand scheme of things becomes a new
normality. Many sociologists in the early twentieth century all pointed
to the fact that with a new world and culture arising, with fast paced
economic transition and urbanization from the slower agricultural
economy to industrialization, the *relative* security and habits of the old
world were discarded, and man were finding it hard to find himself in
the new economy, he was being *alienated*.[176, 177]

Their analysis of the contemporary culture of the early twentieth
century was constructive as the noted fatigue was viewed as the human
body's refusal to adopt to the pressures of the early industrial economy
with its mundane assembly lines. Thus, it was regarded as a limit that
had been broken, a physical signal and response calling for adequate

---

[176]Weber, Max. *Essays in Economic Sociology* (Princeton: Princeton University
Press; First edition, translated, 1999).

[177]Durkheim, Emile. *The Division of Labour in Society* (New York: Free Press,
translated, 1997).

periods of rest and recreation. The fatigue symptoms were seen as a yearning manifest to lawmakers to create better conditions for workers and thereby serving the greater societal interest by contravening the risk for societal collapse.[178]

Eventually these cultural diseases tend to evaporate; after World War I, the number of cases of hysteria and the general fatigue syndrome dropped significantly as during the *Roaring Twenties* with its booming economy, fatigue and a gloomy mood was no longer *en vogue* and came to vanish from public discourse. However, the symptoms never completely ceased to exist, some simply migrated to newly minted psychiatric or medical ailments, and the late 1930s again saw a rise in fatigue related symptoms corresponding with the Great Depression. In current parlance, the general fatigue syndrome is labelled *occupational burnout* which has seen epidemic increases, and the root cause is assumed to be increased stress as the world again is experiencing a shifting economy with automation and knowledge focus putting exceeding pressure on ever greater numbers of workers.

---

[178]Johannisson, Karin. "Trötthetens problem har gamla anor" (*Svenska Dagbladet* 29 November 2002).

CHAPTER 6
THE DEATH DRIVE IN FORCE

Civilisations die from suicide, not by murder.

— Arnold J. Toynbee, British historian (1889-1975)

The above quote by influential British historian Arnold J. Toynbee concluded his insights from one of his most famous works, the voluminous *A Study of History* reviewing the rise and fall of 23 civilizations. He found that civilizations arise from small groups, mostly bound together through bloodlines, taking on great challenges, such as conquering new land, and if successful they established new civilizations. Their demise, he deduced was rarely due to succumbing to external threats by some other emerging civilization, but rather because the successful means with which they had developed their empires in the first place now had vanished, he referred to it as a *product of wills*. This conquering mentality that existed at the onset of the expanding civilization had become muted and its absence was what over time brought the civilization down. This as the previously so dynamic and entrepreneurial elite no longer carries the favorable psychological characteristics but has regressed into a risk averse mode, with the only aspiration of hanging onto money and power. To Toynbee, it was evident that it was the spiritual (psychological) dimension that had faded.[179]

Whereas some civilizations dissipate through extended economic difficulties, often due to genetic impoverishment over the generations manifested through sinking revenues and ever-increasing welfare costs hard to cut without risking revolts, only a few of them actually collapse due to bankruptcy. And whilst the economy might no longer be at its peak, at the time of the collapse it is far from being in doldrums, so tracking economic indicators as pre-cursor signals to a societal downfall will not provide forecasting accuracy as they do not serve as proxies for mental stagnation. However, adverse psychological conditions can be picked up through other metrics, including:

Suicide rates,

Levels of mental ill-health,

Alcoholism/Drug Abuse, and,

Life expectancy.

However, with the exception of life expectancy, these statistics come with quite significant measurement problems, and their interpretations are not always straight forward, as the things they represent often carry stigma and bad will. Hence, it is not unusual for regimes with the power to influence their bureaucracies to sometimes prevent an em-

---

[179]Toynbee, Arnold J. *A Study of History, Vol. 1: Abridgement of Volumes I-VI and Vol. 2: Abridgement of Volumes VII-X* (New York: Oxford University Press; Revised ed. Edition, 1987).

barrassing statistic from being reported or enforce changes to its definition so that to study the trend is no longer possible, even going so far as to outright falsify statistics to reverse negative trends. There are however supranational organizations, most notably the World Health Organization (WHO), that standardize definitions and collect data from member states on an annual basis which provides more reliable statistics that can be used for cross-country trend analysis.

Suicide has long been linked to alienation, sometimes prompted through urbanization and secularization, and seasonal patterns have been documented with summers and public holidays having the highest frequencies of suicides. Interestingly enough, levels of suicide go down during war times but, as expected, correlates with economic depressions. Men generally commit suicide more frequently than women, up to three to four times more common, although in China women commit more suicide than men. Single and childless people commit more suicides than married ones and parents.[180]

Given the many taboos that often surround suicide, it tends to be underreported in many countries, not unusually registered as single car accidents or drowning accidents when in fact they were suicides. Albeit this affects the total numbers, trends over time are nevertheless useful statistics to study changes in frequency and attempting to correlate them to societal events that might influence the numbers.

Leading up to World War I, and aligned with the expanding industrialism and urbanization, suicides in Europe increased drastically, in

---

[180]Baudelot, Christian; Establet, Roger. *Suicide: The Hidden Side of Modernity* (Cambridge, United Kingdom; Polity Press, 2008).

France from 10 per 100,000 inhabitants to almost 25 between 1860 and 1900, in Britain from 6 to 12 per 100,000 inhabitants during the same time. The large difference in numbers between the countries was due to different measurement definitions, however the trends all pointed in the same direction.[181]

Also, mental ill-health carries a conspicuous stigma in many countries, and thus one must assume cases being under-reported making cross-country comparisons difficult but the metrics can also deviate within a country/culture over the decades as the definitions of what constitutes mental illnesses differ and generally have expanded considerably over time. Albeit that in itself can arguably be a sign of a mentally stagnating society and therefore need not skew the statistics. In some countries such as in the former Soviet Union, certain mental illnesses, like *sluggish schizophrenia*, were part of the political psychiatry and dissidents could be punished by being locked up in psychiatric wards accused of being mentally ill because of their political views. But again, to declare certain political views as equivalent to mental illnesses is a sign of the repressiveness in society and would therefore also not distort the trend analysis.

However, one needs to distinguish cases where prolonged economic depressions lead to psychological ailments and cause a surge in suicides as a result of high unemployment numbers, personal bankruptcies, or other economic difficulties. So, adverse psychological developments can occur without a death drive activating, however these increases tend to recede hastily as economic conditions improve and can

---

[181]Ibid.

therefore be differentiated. To consider the death drive as the causal factor, the increasing trends in deteriorating demographic metrics need therefore to transcend the economic cycle.

As a heterogeneous society can harbor many trends at the same time, some contradicting each other, drastic changes must occur to activate a death drive and it must play out over a significant portion of the population to be statistically observed. And these metrics need to point in concert to decreasing general levels of psychological well-being, in that sense it will work as a timing device to indicate when a death drive has activated.

A Turn to Destruction – Radicalization

What follows after an extended period of stagnation that has been allowed to linger on and causes psychologically detrimental effects is *radicalization*. Anecdotal evidence points to changes in the shared perception of reality as the spark to the inception of what was previously regarded as an unlikely set of actions. Something must have prompted a change in the collective mindset that suddenly opens the mental door for the acceptance, or at least passive endorsement, of a profound break of existing norms and social codes, often including an escalating element of destructiveness and violence. Thus, we need to look at cases where the perception of the proverbial cup as half full *changes* to half empty, in essence where confronting the existing order with destructive behavior becomes a conceivable path of recourse. Such a sudden transition from abiding the reigning norms into a pathological mood might however often appear puzzling. But in accordance with the death drive concept, the bursts of destructive displays can be seen as attempt to address an impaired psychological situation by externalizing and articulating what has been repressed in the collective unconscious. As such, the risk of radicalization is higher in a psychologically repressive society, which does not necessarily need to equal a political dictatorship, but rather a society that is culturally and morally withdrawn with conflicts arising when the conscious becomes limited due to what the reigning norms will allow for and the unconscious is having to harbor an increasing number of taboos.

So, whilst structural factors do play a role in explaining societal destruction and need to be assessed and understood, without a psychological trigger the likelihood of violent outbursts remains low. But, as these psychological forces emerge from the unconscious, the adopted explanatory factors rest with structural deficiencies, whether of a political, ethnic, economic, or religious nature. And it has become a self-serving and comfortable deception that the general public never wants to engage in conflict, perpetually peace loving by nature, and that they are somehow being tricked into it by scheming politicians and greedy business interests. However, concerted efforts to provoke conflicts with a pent-up release of aggressions have been demonstrated to hold therapeutic qualities. Hence, notions on what is considered 'good' or 'bad' must here be defined from a psychological perspective and how various mental environments affect mankind. Any moral considerations of good and bad can therefore not be viewed as fixed or absolute values, but they are relative and conditioned by how society performs in terms of psychological well-being.

Hallmarks of Radicalization

As radicalism enters the collective mindset, it is accentuated by a set of truths that cannot be questioned, which have evolved in the repressive atmosphere, underpinned by the typical religious sacraments, even in a non-religious context; the strict set of rituals, a defined *Messiah*, *Heaven* and *Hell* with its *Devil*. With the Hell represented through the many social taboos that have evolved, the Devil being projected into scapegoats and being appeased through various rituals of sacrifice. These works are temporary releases of psychological pressure that has built-up. Just the mentioning of contentious topics brings noted signs of anxiety and an ever-increased vocabulary of euphemisms are required to describe and gloss over undesired aspects of reality, in essence a liturgical language evolves.

As the radicalization phase commences, the newly radicalized proactively seek confrontation and conflict rather than avoiding it, no longer sidestepping or even deliberately ignoring issues that previously would have been brushed aside and repressed. The radicalized come to act with no intent for compromise and operate on a black and white worldview where all blame is directed against a spelled out and well-defined enemy. The fanaticism tends to increase with the hopelessness of the situation. In that sense, destruction rather than being victorious is what fuels the behavior and can be characterized as the uncompromising sect like behavior, such as:

Aggression, any critique is vehemently dismissed;

Aversion towards outsiders;

Alienation, and;

Absolute truth.[182]

Radicalization aims to reject the governing political power by undermining its foundation, in which violence serves as one means to an end. It is often claimed that one only radicalizes toward extreme ideas or ideals but that must be relativized *vis-a-vis* the status quo it is targeting. From the perspective of the ruling ideology though, the idea to radicalize will always be deemed as extreme and sometimes also irrational.[183]

The path towards radicalization has been a continuous matter of debate and a number of theories have developed. Studies show that a radicalized rarely meets the definition of a psychopath, but certain psychological factors can play a role:

- Emotional vulnerability;

- Dissatisfaction with the status quo of (political) activism or protests; and

- Accommodating a narrative exacerbated through a polarizing propaganda.[184]

---

[182]Nylund, Karl-Erik. *Att leka med elden: Sekternas värld* (Sverige: Selling & Partner, 2., omarb. uppl., 2004).

[183]Wilner and Dubouloz. "Homegrown terrorism and transformative learning: an interdisciplinary approach to understanding radicalization" *Global Change, Peace, and Security* 22:1 (2010). p. 38.

[184]Pape, Robert. *Dying to Win: The Strategic Logic of Suicide Terrorism* (New York: Random House. 2005).

Some count over a dozen different theories to radicalization, however the death drive concept is rarely considered, and there exists no single theory in mainstream academia that solely can explain the reasons behind it. But given that the death drive intrinsically seeks to undermine and destroy the status quo, including allowing for a mindset ready to endorse and deploy violent means, the psychological causes for it to activate corresponds well to the radicalization process.

As the death drive operates through shared psychological mechanisms, its motivation underpins the establishment of radical political or religious movements as vehicles to propel the destruction of what obstructs the desired change. But as Freud posited, its rationale is merely a process to rectify a mentally unsound environment, so the ulterior motives of its manifestations, including radicalism and terrorism are not driven by genuine political or religious convictions, it merely superfluously appears so. This must not, however, be interpreted as all radical movements or terrorist organizations are *only* psychological responses, but they do point to psychological problems in a society that need to be addressed with remedial actions, including ensuring that repressed and suppressed material be treated consciously rather than regarded as taboos and excluded from the discourse and public debate.

Some radicalization pathways suggested by academia occur collectively,[185] *group grievance* being such phenomena where a shared, either perceived or legitimately inflicted, injustice or trauma has evolved into a symbolic event around which a group can identify. Such group grievances are clustered around political, religious, or ethnic sentiments, and

---

[185]McCauley, Clark; Moskalenko, Sophia. *Friction: How Radicalization Happens to Them and Us* (New York: Oxford University Press, 2011).

whilst individual members themselves might never have been exposed to the injustice in question, they still can take radical action on behalf of the group. As the radicalization phase is nearing with the deployment of violent means becoming a feasible option, typically the movement splits into factions divided over its use, i.e. terrorism versus non-violent activism. Both factions will over time demand loyalty from their members and thus further radicalize the more extreme viewpoints, and for some members it becomes the exit point and they leave the movement entirely. Hence, only supporters within the movement will proceed to conduct radicalized acts, whereas proxy sympathies and actions by outsiders on behalf of the movement remain rare.[186] So, by belonging to a collective that becomes radicalized, it can thereby trigger radicalization among individual members that otherwise would not have occurred, as the process strengthens a collective's identity under circumstances of duress.

As a society gets ready to engage in collective violence, whether internally and externally directed, a *war fever* tends to precede it, where the hurdle to accept mass killings has been relaxed. To work up a collective into a frenzy where aggression and destruction come to the psychological forefront, but also feelings of fear, heated up to a pathological fervor often by a leadership labelled paranoid or pathological by later historians. Terms like *psychic numbing* describe well the conditions where the adoption of increasingly violent and provocative vocabulary

---

[186]Wood, Vincent. "British Muslim leader says May MUST crack down on prison radicalisation to beat terror," *Sunday Express*, March 25, 2017.

to describe reality is on the rise, and as such becomes objectively measurable.[187]

Scapegoats and Monsters

In a repressive environment, the scapegoat toward which feelings of aggressions will be directed, will always be the individuals that for one reason or another refuse to side with the reigning doctrine. Often it is the independent thinker, as he with ease sees through the simplicity and naivety of the propaganda and its limited worldview of such often vulgar campaigns highlighted by simplistic slogans, and with wit can expose the absurdities in an ironic manner. Intellectuals, typically highly cognitive individuals, will by definition always be under suspicion given their ability to autonomous thought, and parroted platitudes at some level will come to their notice with the outspoken and rebelliously inclined ones having a hard time resisting pointing out their flaws through ridicule.

As previously highlighted, by reviewing the content of various art forms and noting the increased frequency of portraying monsters and the generally grotesque as a mean to defeat the meaninglessness of stagnation, it serves as an interesting point of study as their characteristics highlight the aversion themes in society. What the monstrosity represents will differ; in that sense, they are transformative figures, the time epoch decides what it is that is considered freakish and morally unfit, and it comes to be epitomized by the monster. The monster depiction

---

[187]Lifton, Robert Jay. "Beyond psychic numbing: a call to awareness," *American Journal of Orthopsychiatry*, October, 1982, 52 (4).

contrasts the reigning normality through its psychological and ideological features, often displayed in a highly visually manner. The monster has both a productive and disturbing role as it reflects collective fears, hopes, and desires, and at the same time, it protects us from losing our self-image as inner deviations can be projected on the scapegoat monster. Hence, the monster serves as a useful vehicle to gauge a society's taboos and contrasts with what the ideal representations are; in essence, the monster captures the difference between *us and them*. Throughout history, typically a deformed body has come to represent moral deficiency, and political and social uncertainty. In the late nineteenth century, bearded ladies, dwarfs, non-whites, and lunatic loners came to represent the bizarre and were often displayed at *vaudeville* freak shows. But the Victorian era also witnessed the character of monsters starting to evolve from the deformed body to the deformed human mind, *Dr. Jekyll and Mr. Hyde* serving as the literary case in point. With that transformation, the monster could reside within you, it was no longer easy to point out who the monster was through a visual inspection as it came down to character, much coinciding with the progress of psychology as an independent academic discipline.[188]

But are monsters and scapegoats created for the sole purpose of destroying them, i.e. are they an integral part of the death drive, and as such come to be defined as representing the elements of status quo that the death drive seeks to destroy? To Freud, horror by the monstrous is explained as the return of repressed perceptions, i.e. taboos. To handle

---

[188]Wright, Alexa. *Monstrosity: The Human Monster in Visual Culture* (London, United Kingdom: I.B. Tauris & Co. Ltd, 2013).

this repressed material, projections provide temporary relief as a cleanliness process of sorts, where perceptions of reality harbored in one's own unconscious and deemed impure can be projected onto others and thus a feeling of purity can be achieved. The scapegoat groups that become affiliated with these perceptions turn into victims of verbal forms of hate, rage, witch hunts, and persecutions that usually end in violence of different forms. Scapegoating can be defined as a *"process in which the mechanisms of projection or displacement are utilised in focusing feelings of aggression, hostility, frustration, etc., upon another individual or group; the amount of blame being unwarranted."*[189]

The scapegoats will be blamed for any mishaps or misfortunes extending to conspiracy theories, and even accused as culprits to natural disasters and random accidents, the blame game will be *legion*. Demonization and dehumanization are frequently used to detach scapegoats from the general community. Dehumanization comes in many forms and can occur at an institutional level down to the individual. It takes various expressions, such as likening the scapegoat to animals ("they live like pigs"), symbolic form, with comparisons to various types of imagery ("they look like pigs"), or physical form, from outright violence down to refusal to make eye contact.[190]

---

[189]Mondofacto.com, "Scapegoating," www.mondofacto.com/ (accessed January 1, 2019)

[190]Haslam, N. "Dehumanization: An Integrated Review," *Personality and Social Psychology Review* 10, 2006, pp. 252-264.

Radicalization Preceding World War I

World War I came to mark the *grand finale* of the Victorian era, and to Freud, the mass slaughters and modern warfare on an industrial scale made him consider it as the workings of a death drive, but not only to him, many contemporary accounts from the outbreak of the war witnessed that celebrations and a sense of joy and relief were common, spontaneous manifestations, in essence, *people were looking forward to going to war*. By all accounts, and with the concepts of honor and glory being held in high esteem, the number of deserting soldiers was very low during the first years of the war, up to 1917, despite exceptionally high mortality and injury rates. And transcending the themes of honor and glory was the promise of adventure, as well as to both spiritually and literally battle the cultural decadence that abhorred many; in all, a war psychosis formed through the radicalization process, a massive collective urge to destruction triggered by the death drive. In other words, could it be that the repressive Victorian moral and social norms adhered to across Europe were to blame for the outbreak of the war rather than some of the standard explanations? That this was due to a power struggle of chasing colonies and gaining market shares? To many historians, acknowledged rule-of-thumbs have been that wars rarely start in economically prosperous times and between democracies, however World War I occurred when the European continent, including Russia, was in an intense phase of industrialization, with booming economies and low levels of unemployment. And the main combatants, Britain, France, Germany, and Austria-Hungary, whilst not Russia, were all aspiring democracies where most men, if not yet women, had the right to vote and social democratic parties had entered the political arena standing up for working class interests. So, from an economic and political perspective, nothing pointed to the outbreak of war, yet when it was declared it was met with genuine excitement, testified to by contemporary eyewitness accounts.

As much of the psychological environment was controlled and constrained through rigid Victorian values, also adhered to in continental Europe, the outlook for a war was seen by many as a quest for authenticity, and a search for true spirituality against the features that Victorian culture had implicitly endorsed, including materialism, banality, hypocrisy, and rationality. It was a cultural cleansing process. The cultural elite promoted these sentiments confronted the leading political and business interests, and themes such as eerie mysticism and the death motif in both art and literature were dominant when compared to previous eras. War was seen as a liberating act against the small-minded attitudes of bourgeois lifestyle and preferences.[191]

In today's terms one would label the Victorian era as an extreme form of political correctness with anything even vaguely touching on sexuality in the public discourse being taboo, but under the surface, the hypocrisy was enormous as prostitution and venereal diseases were rampant. The approach to censorship took on almost farcical characteristics; English physicist Thomas Bowdler (1754-1825) took it upon himself to publish a censored version of William Shakespeare's works, cleansed from perceived vulgarism, and the Bible also came under his

---

[191]Eksteins, Modris. *Rites of Spring* (Boston: First Mariner Books edition 2000, orig 1989).

scrutiny, as he suggested the need for a heavily sanitized version, which eventually came to naught.[192]

The repressive creed in European countries was so suffocating that it was a main factor, in addition to economic opportunities, to the mass migration to the United States. Some countries, such as Sweden, saw more than 20 percent of the population depart.

While the economic development and level of innovations were unprecedented, the modern world with its industrialism carried hallmarks of decadence and degeneracy, and not only the cultural *avant-garde* but the broader masses of the population were looking for a cultural rebirth to something considered more 'pure.' The outbreak of a war brought with it the opportunity to do a great reset of cultural institutions and practices. Many segments of the population came to the realization that the destruction of the existing world was a pre-requisite for the development of a better one. Some referred to it as a *"revolt against intellect"* and a longing back to the cohesive community of the agricultural villages versus the alienation created through urbanization and technology. The blood sacrifices on the battlefields were seen as part of the purification process on the way to a better world. Thus, terms like *baptism through fire* was a ritual passage for a second birth of sorts. These daydreams of a utopia instead of the anonymity of the factories filled millions with fantasies; in that sense, it resonated with Freud's view of war as a vehicle to handle repressed material, and thus releasing the

---

[192]Perrin, Noel; Godine, David R. *Dr. Bowdler's Legacy: a history of expurgated books in England and America* (Boston: Nonpare, 2nd ed 1992, orig 1969).

anxiety feelings where even the possibility of one's own demise carried purifying properties for society as a whole.[193, 194]

Case Study – The Fall of Communism in Eastern Europe

The fall of communism in Eastern Europe took everyone by surprise. There had been very few, really no predictions of its demise, surprisingly given that the monitoring and assessment of the USSR and its satellite states deployed thousands of analysts, not only working for Western intelligence organizations but also in academia, the media, think tanks, and for various business interests. These *Kremlinologists* had, in various degrees, access to official statistics and records of shifting quality in terms of accuracy, sometimes being deliberately distorted, even falsified, satellite photos, so-called *humint*, gathered intelligence including clandestinely collected from various sources. Yet, leading up to the events of 1989 with the fall of the Berlin Wall and subsequently the dissolution of the USSR in 1991, historians struggled to find any credible and consistent forecasts that correctly predicted the downfall. *Au contraire*, reading publicly available intelligence reports in the years leading up to the debacle provide no hints of what was to come, in fact,

---

[193]Griffin, Roger. "The Meaning of 'Sacrifice' in the First World War," paper adapted from: Griffin, R., *Modernism and Fascism* (New York: Palgrave Macmillan, 2007). https://www.libraryofsocialscience.com/essays/griffin-the-meaning/index.html (accessed January 1 2019).

[194]Freud. Sigmund; Einstein, Albert. *Why War? A Correspondence Between Albert Einstein and Sigmund Freud* (Published by the Peace Pledge Union with the permission of the International Institute of Intellectual Co-operation of the League of Nations, 1939).

the minor changes in their content make these annual reviews difficult to distinguish one year from another; it appears to have mostly been copy-paste work from previous editions. But it was not easy to predict as the dissolution of the Soviet Union and its ideological empire was remarkable in that it was not preceded by a violent revolution like that of 1917, no sudden *coup d'etat*, or as a consequence of a significant military loss. So, conventional wisdom discounted the possibility of an imminent collapse.

But how did it come that one of the superpowers came to such a sudden end? Its armed forces with its nuclear capacity was only outmatched by its main opponent, the United States. The Soviet Union saw very little domestic political opposition, the state had developed an enormous apparatus to control its population, and while there had been some political uprisings in the satellite states over which it had considerable influence, these had been largely subdued by the Soviet military stepping in and crushing them. The 1980 summer Olympics in Moscow became a show piece of what appeared to be a well-functioning country. And communism as a political ideology, especially among the younger generation in the West, albeit only a *very* vocal minority, was regarded favorably, especially in the 1970s, with the economies experiencing a severe economic depression in the aftermath of the oil crisis with high youth unemployment. Influential left-wing terrorist groups, such as the *Rote Armee Fraktion*, were endorsed, aspiring by force of arms to crush the capitalist system in the West.

However, there were some dark clouds on the horizon; the Soviet invasion of Afghanistan in 1979 eventually turned out to be their equivalent of the U.S. war experience in Vietnam, and the high cost of keeping pace in the arms race was taking a toll on the economy, which through its state planned command economy proved hard to deliver the desired goods and services efficiently and sufficiently to its consumers, a phenomenon exacerbated by corruption at anemic levels.

Around 1975, the USSR entered a period of economic slowdown in which it would remain until its demise. This has become one of mainstream academia's key explanatory root causes to the downfall, an economy that could not grow fast enough due to it lacking the capitalist demand-supply market mechanism and was further subdued by the increasing military spending in the arms race with the West. But, this explanation does not quite stand up, the USSR was far from bankruptcy and, while the economy had been slowing down, it was not in doldrums, at least not according to the official statistics that have since largely been corroborated. Nowhere did it point to a looming collapse of the whole society. From 1974 to 1984 the growth rate (GDP per capita) was on average 0.93 percent per annum, further slowing down with the onset of *perestroika* to minus 1.3 percent annually as efforts to transform the economy was initiated, altogether lower than what it had been from the 1950s up to the mid-1970s, averaging 3.6 percent annually. The budget deficit was less than 2 percent of GDP in 1985, and although it grew to almost 9 percent in 1989, it was still not a dramatic number.[195, 196]

But what was striking to foreign visitors to the USSR and the other Eastern Bloc countries was the dullness and how lifeless these societies

---

[195]Maddison, Angus. *The World Economy. Volume 2: Historical Statistics* (Paris, France: Development Centre Studies - OECD, 2006) pp. 478-479.

[196]Heleniak, Tim; Motivans, Albert. "A Note on Glasnost' and the Soviet Statistical System" (*Soviet Studies*, Vol. 43, No. 3, 1991) pp. 473-490.

appeared, they lacked that dynamic vibrant feel and much of their citizen's lifestyles were bogged down by state bureaucracy which in effect prevented most individual and private initiatives. Whilst Russian culture excelled in all artistic areas and indeed could truly be labelled a *high culture*, the contemporary Soviet cultural life was largely stale, with new productions being nowhere close to match the previous splendors. The art scenes were mostly performing the old classics, and not seldom with a Marxist twist, and the genre of *social realism*, produced only kitsch like lifeless exhibits to promote political axioms which in some Eastern Europe countries eventually came to evolve into acts of subversive affirmation as a way of protest. This as the political propaganda and platitudes appeared increasingly detached from everyday life, the lies that formed the political doctrine forced much aspects of reality to be blanked out and disregarded, blind spots appeared everywhere as people had to pretend that certain parts of life simply did not exist, such as when official news bulletins talked about economic progress whilst the queues for everyday necessities grew longer.[197, 198]

One of the few that had discussed the possibility of the USSR collapsing was French historian Emmanuel Todd in his *La chute finale: Essais sur la décomposition de la sphère Soviétique* from 1976. While not precise in the timing of such a dissolution and not alluding to the Freudian death drive, he referred to many displays that carry the hallmarks of the

---

[197]Havel, Vaclav. *En dåre i Prag : brev, tal, texter 1975-1990* (Stockholm, Sweden; Symposion, transl. Karin Mossdal, 1990).

[198]Malia, Martin. *Russia under Western Eyes: From the Bronze Horseman to the Lenin Mausoleum* (Cambridge; Belknap Press of Harvard University Press, 2000).

death drive. He studied demographic statistics such as infant mortality rates, life expectancy, and suicide rates, all of which painted a disturbing picture of a society in decline and highlighted how these reflected the passive attitudes reigning not only among the population, but also the leadership. Todd described how the sentiment of the Soviet elite had started to shift in the early 1960s as a result of recognizing the limitations of the communist system in delivering the ambitions set-out in the 5-year plans, and that they had, implicitly at least, given up with the mere focus of protecting their privileges, merely clinging on to shallow slogans that were increasingly disjoined with conditions on the ground.[199]

With declining life expectancy, raging alcoholism, and increased levels of suicide, all due to the same psychological root cause, the statistics highlighted a population that had given up on the system, and through radicalized means embarked on a path of collective self-destruction, as such the societal edifice withered away and when the resignation had reached its end point, it self-destructed. While violence levels in the Soviet bloc were muted, with the exception of Yugoslavia, as compared to before the revolution of 1917, the destructive tendencies of the death drive were turned inwards with distinctly increased levels of suicide and a shrinking life span. As such, the dismissal nature of the status quo revealed itself not through violent protests and uprisings, but from inside the communist party itself, with a new leadership that sought, through reforms, an internal revolution of sorts, to break the

---

[199]Todd, Emmanuel. *The Final Fall: An Essay on the Decomposition of the Soviet Sphere* (New York: Karz Publishers, transl 1979, orig 1976).

stagnation that was frustrating the whole society and attempted to reverse the population trends that clearly had embarked on a path to self-destruction. The effects on the status quo were, however, much the same, it collapsed under a reformist chosen to lead the communist party by seeking to liberalize not only the economy but by challenging and undermining the whole Soviet mindset. Mikhail Gorbachev attacked what he saw as a moral decline, a degeneration that was causing reprobate behavior and lethargy in most areas of Soviet life. He sought a moral uprising and was quoted in an interview as saying:

> *The Soviet model was defeated not only on the economic and social levels; it was defeated on a cultural level. Our society, our people, the most educated, the most intellectual, rejected that model on the cultural level because it does not respect the man, oppresses him spiritually and politically.*[200]

Through instilling a new mindset, a shift in perceptions, what previously were blind spots, weaknesses in the system that no one pretended were there, they became visible and blatant, provoking a call for change by now openly questioning the existing arrangements. The collective mindset had changed with drastic consequences infused with a crave for revolutionary change.

---

[200] Aron, Leon. *Everything You Think You Know About the Collapse of the Soviet Union Is Wrong* (Foreign Policy, 20 June 2011) https://foreignpolicy.com/2011/06/20/everything-you-think-you-know-about-the-collapse-of-the-soviet-union-is-wrong/ (accessed January 1 2019)

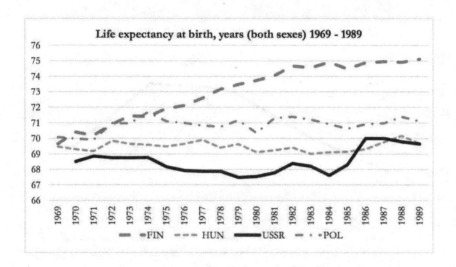

Figure 1) Life expectancy at birth, years (both sexes) 1969 - 1989. USSR, Finland, Hungary & Poland. Source: WHO European Health for All database (HFA-DB) https://gateway.euro.who.int/en/datasets/european-health-for-all-database/

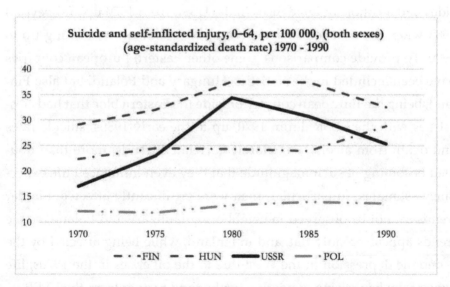

Figure 2) Suicide and self-inflicted injury, 0–64, per 100 000, (both sexes) (age-standardized death rate) 1970 - 1990. USSR, Finland, Hungary & Poland. Source: WHO European Health for All database (HFA-DB) https://gateway.euro.who.int/en/datasets/european-health-for-all-database/

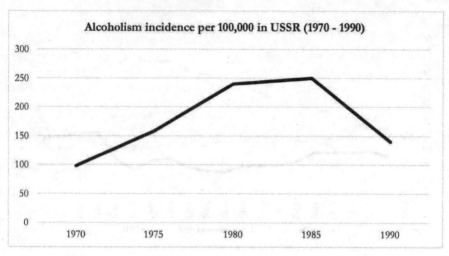

Figure 3) Alcoholism incidence per 100,000 in USSR (1970 - 1990). Source:
https://clinmedjournals.org/articles/iaarm/international-archives-of-addiction-research-and-medicine-iaarm-2-018.pdf

Figures 1-3 provide insights on the trends of life expectancy, suicides and alcoholism incidences in the USSR from 1970 up and beyond 1985 when the first reforms of perestroika commenced, leading up to 1990. To provide comparisons, some other Eastern European countries have been included in the statistics, Hungary and Poland, but also Finland, being the European country outside the Eastern bloc that had closest ties with the USSR. From 1970, up to the early 1980s, suicide rates and death from alcoholism, closely correlated trends, more than doubled becoming of such magnitude that they even influenced life expectancy estimates. In particular, men were significantly affected. Similar trends cannot be observed in neighboring Hungary and Poland, as the trends appear broadly flat, and in Finland, while being affected by the economic depression in the West due to the oil crises in the 1970s, life expectancy kept rising, deviating further and further from the USSR.

In 1985, there is a noted break in the upward trends for suicide and alcohol related deaths in the USSR, the government finally reacting to the severities of the numbers and instituting campaigns to curb the abuse of alcohol, withdrawing supply and promoting a sober lifestyle. The trend shows an almost immediate reversal, the question of how 'massaged' that statistics were, if at all, to present a successful campaign, can be argued. At any rate, the effect was only temporary, after the dissolution of the USSR in 1991, throughout the 1990s the trends were yet again increasing at alarming levels. Thus, the 1970s was the decade that the death drive activated in the USSR and by the mid-1980s the insight that the country faced self-destruction had been duly noted by the leadership, but attempts at reform by the communist party to break the detrimental effects of the death drive were too little and definitely too late, instead these in themselves only came to hasten the collapse of communism in Eastern Europe.

Case Study - The Arab Spring

The Arab Spring quite literally ignited in December 2010 in Tunisia when a street vendor set himself on fire to protest against corruption and police brutality. The self-immolation triggered further protests in Tunisia, eventually provoking a revolution. However, the protests were not confined to Tunisia but spread across North Africa and the Middle East, affecting countries such as Bahrain and Egypt severely, while seeing its most violent expressions in Libya, Syria and Yemen where it escalated to full-scale civil wars. Although the events collectively came to be labelled the Arab Spring, it also spread outside the Arab world however within the Muslim sphere. But the corruption and state brutality that superficially were deemed as the cause inciting the protests and violence were nothing new in the region; it was so common place that it was part of everyday life. Why did then the Arab Spring occur when it did, and why did an isolated incident in Tunisia spread across the region so quickly and at such a widespread scale when the underlying root causes been there for decades, even centuries? In fact, the Arab Spring was so all encompassing that it was the biggest political uprising in the region since the wave of decolonization some 50 years earlier.

By early 2012, long standing dictators such as Muammar Gaddafi in Libya had been toppled, the political leadership in Egypt, Tunisia, and Yemen had also been overthrown. However, and with some noted exceptions, by mid-2012, the revolutionary fervor had succumbed and many of the sitting governments had managed to ride out the storm as the protests had been met with force and counter-movements loyal to the regimes had gathered in strength. But in some countries, the conflict had intensified to civil war, with countries such as Iraq, Libya, Syria, and Yemen experiencing societal collapse.[201]

Whilst similarities have been pointed out between the Arab Spring and the fall of communism in Eastern Europe, in particular how the events and their magnitude took everyone by surprise, they, by and large, came to differ on a main point: the outcomes. In hindsight, and with some of the conflicts still ongoing, the aftermath, which has been dubbed the Arab Winter, produced only somber results as the protes-

---

[201]Brownlee, Jason; Masoud, Tarek; Reynold, Andrew. *The Arab Spring: the politics of transformation in North Africa and the Middle East* (Oxford, United Kingdom: Oxford University Press, 2013).

tors' initial demand for greater democracy and reforms to stifle corruption have mostly not been met; by 2018 only Tunisia had transitioned to a constitutional democracy.[202]

Conventional Explanations

The retrospective conventional explanations for the Arab Spring have been that it was due to the extensive corruption, violent suppression by the authorities against justified demands from the population, and a large part of the demography consisting of youths, particular young males, and that this cohort was susceptible to violent and rowdy demeanors. Whilst youth unemployment was relatively high, the Tunisian economy had been growing at decent rates, in 2010 the real GDP growth rate was 3.5 percent, also Egypt had seen a growing economy with positive numbers during the ten years preceding the protests, see figure 3), and most of the other Arab countries had been experiencing growth. Although unemployment in some areas was high, and the economic windfalls were unevenly undistributed, there was no sign of an impending economic turmoil. So, the protest did not arise out of an ongoing economic depression and whereas the other factors might justify

[202]Alfadhel, Khalifa. *The Failure of the Arab Spring* (Cambridge, United Kingdom: Cambridge Scholars Publishing, 2016).

root causes, they could hardly be the igniting spark, as these had been in place in society for long period.[203, 204]

Albeit the reasons for dissatisfaction must have been there for an extensive period, the existing order was still adhered to and by acting passively implicitly endorsed. However, a psychological impetus must have triggered proceeding the protests that altered the perceptions of reality, which included a desire to attack the status quo and the sitting regimes. And the fact that it spread so quickly with such contagion effects has been attributed to social media, because film clips of protests and appeals to join demonstrations could be shared instantly across the region, but without the will to actively participate among large enough portions of the populations and acting out through street level activism, social media's speedy transmission mechanism would have mattered little. However, it did play an importance to counter state-operated media outlets with an alternate view of events and by lifting the veil off any black-out incidents, and thus influenced the number of active participants.[205]

---

[203]Sullivan, Charles J. "Riding the Revolutionary Wave: America, The Arab Spring and the Autumn of 1989" (*The Washington Review of Turkish and Eurasian Affairs*. Rethink Institute, April 2011).

[204]Brownlee, Jason; Masoud, Tarek; Reynold, Andrew. *The Arab Spring: the politics of transformation in North Africa and the Middle East* (Oxford, United Kingdom: Oxford University Press, 2013).

[205]Friedman, Thomas. "The Other Arab Spring" (*The New York Times*, 7 April 2012).

The differences in fallout between the countries in the region have been widely debated, the protests in Tunisia saw relatively little violence, in particular in comparison to neighboring Libya where the protests developed into a blood drenched civil war. Some analysts have pointed to the various degrees of an educated middle-class presence in the affected countries as a driver for successful change, something which differed between Tunisia and Libya, where the former had it and the latter not, however Syria had for the region a quite affluent middle class yet experienced among the worst bloodletting. Sectarian splits have been pointed out as a differentiator, but also that is an inconsistent characteristic, as Lebanon and Jordan, with noted diversity, saw relatively little conflict due to the Arab Spring.[206]

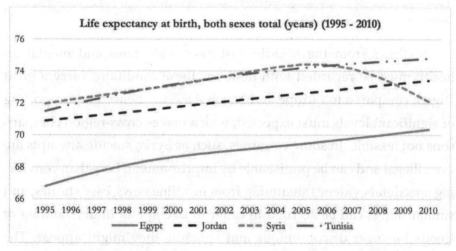

Figure 4) *Life expectancy at birth, both sexes total (years) (1995 - 2010), Egypt, Jordan, Syria & Tunisia. Source: https://data.worldbank.org/indicator/*

[206]Aras, Bülent; Falk, Richard. *Five years after the Arab Spring: a critical evaluation* (Third World Quarterly. 37 (12). 2016) pp. 2252-2258.

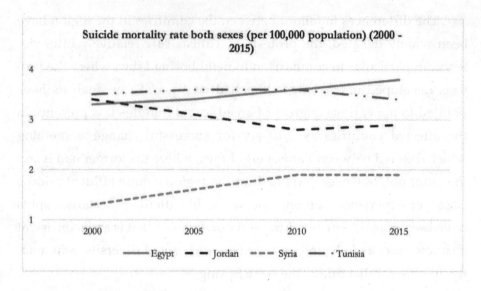

Figure 5) Suicide mortality rate both sexes (per 100,000 population) (2000 - 2015), Egypt, Jordan, Syria & Tunisia.
Source: https://data.worldbank.org/indicator/

Statistics from the Middle East on suicide rates and mental ill-health must be regarded with doubt as these conditions carry a great stigma compared to Europe and North America, hence underreporting of significant levels must expected, which makes cross-region comparisons not feasible. In some countries, such as Syria, suicide attempts are even illegal and can be punishable by imprisonment. Less than convincing anecdotal evidence stemming from headline news, case studies, and similar things can be accrued in order to attempt an understanding of trends however discontinuous and sporadic they might appear. The stigma of psychological disorders has meant that there has been a consistent underspending on mental health facilities, as on surface the problems appear minuscule, even non-existent. And as there more recently have been some recognition thereof, albeit little, and resources are to some extent provided, the number of cases will obviously increase, but whether that reflects or not the underlying trend cannot be ascertained. Some survey points to a 100 percent increase of mental health cases from 1990 up to 2015 in the Eastern Mediterranean region, obviously extending the geography to hinterlands beyond those in particular affected by the Arab Spring and transcending the advent of the violent eruptions in 2010, as such the number can only serve as rough proxy.[207]

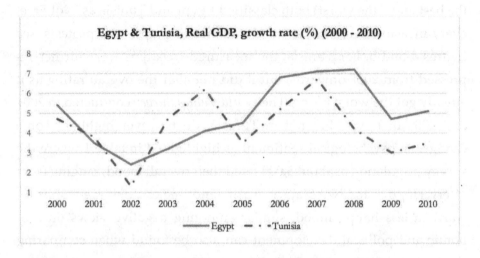

Figure 6) Real GDP with growth rate (%) (2000 - 2010), Egypt & Tunisia. Source: World Bank Development Indicators

Various surveys and indices measuring sentiments and making assessments of the degree of freedom in society would be a potential path to gauge (psychological) repression and stagnation, however only a few of them include the concerning countries and a sufficiently long time period preceding the Arab Spring to be able to perform trend analysis.

---

[207]Mokdad, Ali H.: et al. "The burden of mental disorders in the Eastern Mediterranean region, 1990–2015: findings from the global burden of disease 2015 study" (*Int J Public Health* 63 (Suppl 1). 2018) pp. S25-S37.

The Arab Barometer is one such example, but as the tracking of the key countries in the Arab Spring did not start until 2010 it cannot be deployed to assess changes in sentiments pre-Arab Spring to search for pre-cursors. Surveys that have the sufficient duration and include the affected countries, such as the *Freedom in the World Index*, scoring freedom rating, civil liberties, and political rights from a 1-7 scale (1 being the best and 7 the worst) both classified Egypt and Tunisia as 'Not Free' every measurement year in the decade leading up to the protests, see figures 4 and 5. For Tunisia, the measured freedoms were further repressed from 2007 onwards, but it did not alter the overall rating as it already got the worst rating. The *World Values Survey* conducted in 2001 and 2008 in Egypt, but not in Tunisia, do however highlight some changes in psychological sentiment as highlighted in table 1 where the survey population of about 3,000 rated their overall mood, ranging from "Very Happy" to "Not Happy at All" and one can observe a shift towards a less happy mood, similar emerging negative views on economic and political development can also be found when comparing the 2001 and 2008 results. This divergence between the overall positive macroeconomic indicators, such as GDP growth rates, and a downward shift in mood sentiments provides insight of a certain resentment establishing itself throughout society, yet not starkly manifested in distinctly higher rates of suicide and a lower life expectancy, but if resorting to anecdotal evidence highlighted by alarming numbers of increases in mental ill-health and drug abuse, underlining a growing frustration and providing explanatory power to the out-of-the-blue sudden protests and violent reactions.

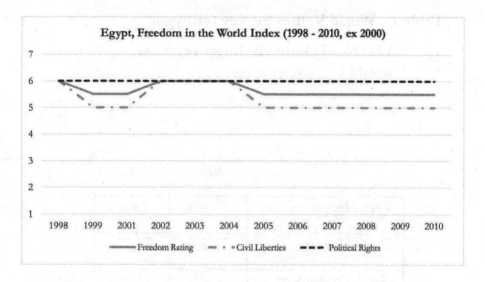

Figure 7) Egypt, Freedom in the World index, Freedom rating, Civil Liberties & Political Rights. 1998 - 2010, ex 2000). Source: https://freedomhouse.org/report/freedom-world/

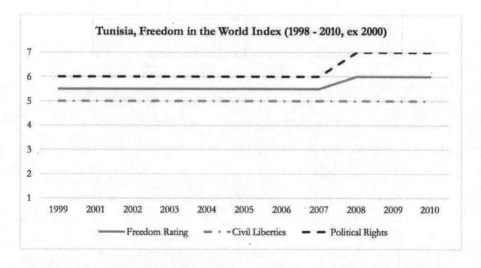

Figure 8) Tunisia, Freedom in the World index, Freedom rating, Civil Liberties & Political Rights. 1998 - 2010, ex 2000). Source: https://freedomhouse.org/report/freedom-world/

Table 1 – World Values Survey for Eygpt

V11/10.- Taking all things together,
would you say you are:

	2001	2008
Very Happy	18.1%	9.6%
Quite Happy	71.3%	73.5%
Not Very Happy	8.8%	14.8%
Not Happy At All	1.6%	2.0%
Don't know	0.2%	0.0%

N=3000   N=3051

CHAPTER 7

HOW TO PREDICT THE DEATH DRIVE

> *Toute dégradation individuelle ou nationale est annoncée par une dégradation proportionnelle dans le langage. (Every individual or national degeneration is revealed by a proportional degradation in language.)*
>
> — *Les Soirées de Saint-Pétersbourg, ou Entretiens sur le gouvernement temporel de la Providence*, Joseph de Maistre (1753-1821) French philosopher

From the case studies, we can outline the phases of the death drive activation process as each of them has defining characteristics and, whilst distinct, they are interwoven and as such succeed each other in a transcending manner. These phases include:

A Psychologically Repressive Environment

A psychologically repressive environment is defined through increasingly dogmatic beliefs that have come to dominate the public discourse, and to openly criticize or confront them comes with the risk of being ostracized or even worse. The restricted narrative increases the taboo areas and to circumvent it, euphemisms are deployed. Slogans and the propaganda used to promote the reigning doctrine become ever simpler and for an outsider incomprehensible as the words used often defy their original meaning, producing nothing but banalities.

Mental Stagnation

With a psychologically repressive environment gaining foothold, a risk averse attitude comes to dominate the population, as the peril of being at odds with the regime is simply too high. Thus, parts of reality are being repressed in an *Emperor's New Clothes* type syndrome. In the end, and as a coping mechanism, people start to give up, and passivity becomes the preferred way of life. As such, mental stagnation kicks in. Over time, there is a noted increase in the number of psychological ailments and also the cases of alcohol and drug abuse reveal alarming trends. In the cultural world, art and literature come to depict the bizarre and morbid, which become a fad attracting a growing number of artist and authors.

Radicalization

To break the status quo, the collective psychology starts to radicalize, seeking disruption and destruction rather than the previous assertive and passive attitude. The world emerges in a black-and-white context with defined scapegoats and confrontational rhetoric. The increasing trend of psychological illnesses has progressed into a surge of suicides. The risk for political violence stands at a high. Either leading politicians will attempt to nip the growing discontent in the bud through reforms, but that often only accelerates the breakdown of the system. Or the regime attempts to quash any protest movements taking form and with that risks escalating into civil war.

In short, the death drive follows a set pattern where the breeding ground is a society or culture whose norms have evolved into something *too* rigid, something unwilling to bend to changing realities, this as certain values have been declared irreproachable and their interpretations have become strict and obstinate. This even when it should be apparent that the resultant outcomes go against any good judgment, any common sense, psychologically it indicates that a certain element of self-delusion is at play. Obviously, the unyielding attitude to adhering to these norms as they have regressed to inflexible edicts of sorts is a more viable prospect in a political dictatorship, where authoritarian leaders can impose their will through means of controlling the state apparatus and media with demands of (self-) censorship, rather than in a pluralistic society. These efforts prompt a doctrine that becomes difficult to confront and challenge. However, such tendencies can also occur in democracies, as over time a set of moral or political standards become so embedded in the mainstream politicians' *repertoire*, usually due to some past debacles or traumas deemed deplorable and as norms are put in place to prevent future similar mishaps. However, over time, given their sanctuary status, they risk becoming unbending and misconstrued, and, in the end, are being conformed to with an almost religious fervor. As the society becomes more restrictive in what it allows to criticize, the number of taboos grows proportionally, forcing aspects of reality to be repressed and suppressed, submerged into the unconscious, with the awareness levels of the population being reduced. Hindsight analysis of the ideologies that come to dominate in stagnating eras appear often surprisingly trite with their simpleton slogans often so watered down in content that they come to mean anything, or rather nothing. The shallow propaganda, which in the objective interpretation only points to a void, in effect highlighting a sterile society, might be the first sign of the death drive activating, as when the dogmatic ideological tenets mindlessly parroted by their most ardent supporters have become so dumbfounded and detached from reality that they are staring into the abyss. In such a pathological environment, psychopaths easily climb the career ladder and come to dominate many senior echelons, further acerbating the mental unbalance of society. The increased levels of infantilism and naivety that forms the political discourse is something which can be assessed and analyzed through the language deployed in publications such as official bulletins and mainstream media. It is observed through more and more topics being painted in black-and-white, turning many into fanatics, as well as growing numbers of taboos that come to blind out parts of reality and having to defer to a growing number of euphemisms to describe the 'unmentionable' and 'unthinkable'.

Eventually, the psychologically repressive environment causes mental stagnation, manifested through increasing numbers of psychological ailments and alcohol/substance abuses. It can also be noted through shifting cultural expressions taking the turn for the bizarre and sinister as projections from the unconscious start to resurface into reality. The depictions of monstrosities and the morbid carry therapeutic properties as they in the form of proxies represent the destruction of status quo. With society facing such a bleak future ahead, and as Freud argued that with death drive acting as catalyst to instigate change to avoid a looming psychological disaster, the collective psychology springs into action through these absurdities. As the death drive emanates from the unconscious, its first acts of revolt will be below the level of human awareness, including inadvertent sabotage of the system but over time the manifestations will be of more tangible nature; suicides become prevalent, to the degree that it might even affect life expectancy numbers. But also, looming political ideas affiliated with taking on and

attacking the sitting regime, often through so-called populist movements, and the risk for political violence, even civil war, has been dramatically heightened. The reigning political leadership in order to cling
on to power might try to instigate reforms, however often in a *too little,
too late* fashion. In the end, the necessary changes to re-balance the mental equilibrium to more sustainable levels are forced through, and the
death drive thus fades out from the collective mindset as it has served
its purpose.

How to Model and Measure the Death Drive?

Once the phases of the death drive, including their characteristics,
have been identified, one can seek out objective metrics to model and
measure it with the aspiration to try to time episodes where the risk for
political violence becomes rampant. Some of these metrics are relatively
straightforward, however as mentioned in the previous chapter, given
their contentious nature at least in certain regions, it is far from certain
that they objectively represent the conditions on the ground, they are
thus marred with measurement problems which could be significant.
Albeit their absolute values might underrepresent the true numbers, the
direction of the trends over time is still likely to be correct, especially, if
all these metrics concur in terms of tendencies.

For the mental stagnation phase, it would include:

Number of cases of mental illnesses;

Number of alcoholism incidences; and

Number of narcotic incidences.

As the final phase enters, further metrics can be added:

Number of suicides; and

Life expectancy.

As evidence of a death drive in force, all of the above metrics should highlight adverse trends over a multi-year time period.

There are however other characteristics of the death drive that must be factored in, but given their elusive nature, proxy metrics must be engaged to track their status, namely cultural themes and the degree of society's repressiveness. While it is universally recognized that the themes and genres that dominate the art scene do vary over time, but with the problems of establishing clear cut definitions, it means that there are no viable mechanisms for tracking them, and thus there exists no index for measurement. To measure psychological repression, there are indeed trackers that attempt to ascertain levels of *political* repression through various freedom indices, however they not granular enough to capture a growing number of taboos that cannot be discussed in the public discourse and to ascertain if the defining values of a nation have become too dogmatic. And obviously one must recognize the difference between political and psychological repression, as the latter might still exist in what by all accounts qualifies as a politically free society. To work around the lack of usable metrics, text analysis of publicly available media outlets transcending the political spectra becomes the preferred method. To be all-encompassing, such analysis and word count need to include metaphors and other symbolic language as well as words, typically adjectives, that displays mood sentiments.

There have been plenty of research on the significance of the language used in various time epochs and situations and how it reflects underlying psychological sentiments, and notably the varying use of metaphor themes. For instance, Lloyd deMause, the American psycho-historian, has been studying the wordings that foreshadow conflicts such as wars and revolutions. He took aim at studying how the military and political leadership deployed particular vocabulary to motivate and mobilize the general population in order to prepare them for war. This included studying any written material from the leadership, extending to include notes of side scribbles, transcripts of speeches highlighting Freudian slips, popular jokes and caricatures of the time. He came, through extensive studies of numerous conflict situations, going back to antiquity up to modern times, to identify a common pattern of a myriad of symbolic references described through various means of figures of speech referring to metaphorical *birth* situations and the distress that surrounds it. He concluded that this was the consistent narrative theme used in how the leadership described reality in pre-conflict situations. Examples included accusations of being choked and strangled by the enemy, and being denied space to live, Adolf Hitler's *Lebensraum* serving as a case in point. There were also plenty of references to caves, tunnels, abysses, and voids that the alluded enemy threaten with, along with the risk of drowning. All referring in one way or another to the pains of the birth process and of being in labor.[208]

But also, the descriptions of a proposed solution to the conflicts were coated in childbirth terminology, including finding a way out of a labyrinth, seeing the light at the end of the tunnel, coming out of the tunnel, and being able to breathe freely again as the enemy has been conquered. Lloyd deMause could identify archetypal strawmen that

[208]deMause, Lloyd. *The New psychohistory* (New York, NY: Psychohistory Press, 1975).

were used in the conflict rhetoric, recurring with prevailing characteristics, including *Stranger, Aggressor, Worthy Opponent, Faceless, Enemy of God, Barbarian, Greedy, Criminal, Torturer, Rapist,* and *Death.* These he argued are seen as projections of repressed perceptions in the unconscious.[209]

So, hence this vocabulary, whilst perhaps rationally seen as a manifest of psychopathology, is in essence the unconscious calling from the death drive wishing to seek destruction and violence, and they become buzz words incorporated by large portions of the masses with the anxiety and anticipations of violence being exacerbated through them. In that sense, a language interspersed with birth metaphors is seeking a rebirth that must be preceded by the death of existing arrangements.

Idioms or figurative language, of which metaphors are a sub-set of, in essence are any grouping of words whose meaning becomes different from that of each word looked at individually, and provide the most fertile ground in finding symbolism. These also include proverbs, parables, analogues, etc., and are a common linguistic tool to describe matters and it exists in all languages. The English language alone contains at least 25,000 idiomatic expressions.[210]

Metaphors provide structures to understand the world. As such, they shape human's pattern of thought, and thus by understanding the themes as they shift and trend over time, as they color and structure our

---

[209]Keen, Sam. *Faces of the Enemy: Reflections of the Hostile Imagination* (New York, NY: Harper & Row, Publishers; first edition, 1991).

[210]Jackendoff, R. *The architecture of the language faculty* (Cambridge, MA: MIT Press, 1997).

perceptions. A metaphor is literary arrangement designed to describe meaning to a situation or object through drawing comparison or associating to something generally completely unrelated in its dictionary meaning to what is being described. Through shared reference the non-literal meaning of the metaphor is understood by the general public.[211] Examples includes:

Life is a journey;

Time is money.

These highlight a common design format of metaphors with a source and a target, with the source, here *journey* and *money*, representing the concepts used to describe or resemble and the target what is being described and understood through the metaphor, in the examples above *life* and *time*.

Metaphors seem to be universal and exist in all known languages, but they are not exclusively used in linguistics; they are also found in other forms of communication, such as artwork and other graphical representations, and even music. Metaphors also exist in extended forms such as anecdotes and parables that provide a broader illustration of the conveyed message.

The common themes metaphors typically consist of include the sources:

The human body (and its characteristics)

---

[211]Lakoff, George P. and Johnson, Mark L. *Metaphors We Live By* (Chicago, IL: University of Chicago, 2nd edition, 2003).

Health and illness

Animals

Plants

Buildings and construction

Machines and tools

Games and sports

Money and economic transactions

Heat and cold

Light and darkness

Forces

Movement and direction[212]

Metaphors are usually applied to describe the targets:

Emotions

Desire

Morality

Thought

Society/Nation

---

[212]Kovecses, Zoltan. *Metaphor, A Practical Introduction* (New York, NY: Oxford University Press, 2nd edition, 2010) Chapter 2.

Economy

Human Relationship

Communication

Time

Life and Death

Religion

Events and Actions[213]

As highlighted in the lists above, metaphors usually go from *concrete to abstract*, describing mental states, groups, processes, and personal experiences, as such using tangibles to describe intangibles.

The relationship between figurative language and its influence on behavior has been studied both from the individual perspective and the collective, especially when applied to advertising, but also to how they influence patients suffering from various psychological conditions. In individual patient cases with behavior considered abnormal or neurotic, it has been demonstrated that such behaviors can be triggered or accentuated through exposure to symbols representing the root of the mental ailments. Typically, it could be if someone has repressed memories of being abused as a child by a person regularly dressed in red colored clothing, in adult life, just the sight of the color red can trigger anxiety in that person due to the fact that the symbolic meaning of red has come to represent pain and abuse. As part of the treatment, it becomes one of the psychoanalyst's main tasks to identify the symbolic

---

[213]Ibid.

meaning of the triggers the release neurosis or similar things. Advertisers and researchers of consumer patterns have long deployed symbols that implicitly or unconsciously relate to motherly comfort, strength and reliability, prestige, sexual appeal, or other typically positive attributes they want to associate with the product they are promoting, these symbols are generally displayed as depictions. However, to date, there seems to be no single generally accepted approach on how to identify symbols that can be understood by their culturally-transmitted meanings and how to link them to archetypes. This fact has been noted within the research community and the ARAS (Archive for Research in Archetypal Symbolism) categorization of archetypal images to which one can attach related symbols probably hitherto serve as the most comprehensive dictionary of symbols in place. The ARAS symbol dictionary can be applied as an initial straw man that with some significant adjustments can be developed to form the base structure of a symbolic language measurement model.[214]

Eventually wider and wider groups of people start to use this figurative language to describe various aspects of everyday life and surroundings and as such they spread and become fashionable and increasingly used, in time, the perceptions change the way reality is being experienced for the broader collective. In that sense, they serve as vehicles that give cues of unconscious wishes and desires, and through being embedded in ideologies and the formative culture and through it channels the distinction between social reality and physical reality.

---

[214]Morrison, Rodger. "New Method of Identifying Archetypal Symbols and their Associated Meanings," *European Journal of Social Sciences*. 27 (2011).

There have been a number of academic studies of the language of the radicalized that highlight a specific vocabulary that sets them apart from non-extremist environments. First and foremost, the radicalization process requires a clearly defined and demonized enemy. This distinction between *us* and *them* prompts black and white jargon with explicit categorical statements and fewer ambiguities, making terms such as 'maybe', 'possibly', perhaps', could be', etc. appear only infrequently. Thus, by employing words that highlights certainties give insights to a personality that is both susceptible to simplification and risk-taking. From that perspective, the usage of certain pronouns will come to the forefront as part of the radicalization process, hence there is a higher frequency of third person plural among extremists, this to highlight and set out 'the other.'[215, 216]

The language of the radicalized also unveils a higher number of words that display negative emotions, including anger and hate, this as they carry a higher engagement to fight for their cause and their discontent with the current status rather than the perceivably lukewarm *average Joe*.[217]

So, an absence of negativities in the language is a sign that radicalism has not commenced. Studies has shown that power terms, including

---

[215]McCauley, C. and Moskalenko, S. *Mechanisms of political radicalization: Pathways toward terrorism* (Terrorism and Political Violence, 20(3), 2008).

[216]Pennebaker, J. W. and Chung, C. K. *Language and social dynamics* (University of Texas at Austin, Technical Report 1318, 2012).

[217]Pennebaker, J. W. and Chung, C. K. "Computerized text analysis of al-Qaeda transcripts" (*The Content Analysis Reader*, K. Krippendorf and M. A. Bock (red), Sage, 2008).

'leader', 'demand,' and 'superior' are common in speeches among American presidents prior to them engaging in armed conflicts, this is also how radicalized convey their message.[218, 219]

Text analysis tools such as Linguistic Inquiry and Word Count (LIWC) are employed to comprehend texts and individual words relation to psychological inclinations and impetus.[220] It has been backed by research that provides evidence that links the use of certain vocabulary to underlying drives and motivations. LIWC provides support in that exercise by providing psychological categories that assist the sorting mechanism. By word counts ranked through relative frequencies profiles of psychological categories can be created. [221, 222]

Once the symbolic words or expressions have been documented and registered they are applied as pick-up filters out from regular reviews of media databases to determine if the occurrences of figurative

[218]Victoroff, J. "The mind of the terrorist a review and critique of psychological approaches," (*Journal of Conflict Resolution*, 49(1), 2005).

[219]Smith, A. G. "From words to action: Exploring the relationship between a group's value references and its likelihood of engaging in terrorism" (*Studies in Conflict and Terrorism*, 27(5), 2004) pp. 409-437.

[220]Pennebaker, J. W.; Francis, M. E. and Booth, R. J. *Linguistic inquiry and word count (liwc): A text analysis program* (New York, NY: Erlbaum Publishers, 2001).

[221]Pennebaker, J.; Mehl, M. and Niederhoffer, K. "Psychological aspects of natural language use: Our words, our selves" (*Annual Review of Psychology*, vol. 54, no. 1, 2003) pp. 547-577.

[222]Tausczik, Y. and P. J.W. "The psychological meaning of words: Liwc and computerized text analysis methods" (*Journal of Language and Social Psychology*, vol. 29, no. 1, March 2010).

languages are increasing or decreasing over time and what themes that are currently popular.

Through the insight from these various studies and by employing the tools for text analysis, including figurative speech, one can detect the language that both pre-empts but also defines the death drive. Thus, incorporating these insights one can now articulate a model that, together with other metrics, distinguishes the various phases of the death drive versus psychologically stable environments.

In the psychologically repressive stage, text analysis of pro-government media and bulletins will highlight over time that the political propaganda and slogans get ever simpler, its wordings turning into banalities, carrying no intelligible meaning. And as the number of taboo areas expand, there is an increased use of euphemism to cover up for the aspects of life that cannot be openly discussed. As the repressive environment further tightens, the frequency of 'certainty' words become prevalent.

As the death drive process progresses into the mental stagnation and radicalization phases, the description of cultural manifestations and phenomena take a turn for the sinister, portrayed in terms of morbidity, monstrosities, perversions, and the bizarre. In the public discourse, as the appetite for destruction and violence increases with the activation of the death drive, symbolic language to interpret reality will be describe through birth process metaphors. Groups targeted as scapegoats will be described in increasingly us-and-them terminology and negative emotion words will be more frequently deployed as are 'power' words.

CHAPTER 8
WAS FREUD ONTO SOMETHING
AFTER ALL?

Мы больше не можем так продолжаться...(we cannot go on like this any longer...)

— Mikhail Gorbachev, General Secretary
of the Communist Party of the Soviet Union, 1985

Societal downfalls do appear to follow a pre-set suite of sequential events that in an escalating mode lead up to the activation of the death drive with the destruction of the societal status quo following in its trail.

So, is the downfall of empires and nations inevitable? History suggests so, hardly any of the historical civilizations have survived. Hence, it appears to be a safe bet that today's countries and cultures will eventually also see their demise. The key issue, however, is the timing of it. More recent events such as the *Fall of Communism in Eastern Europe* and the *Arab Spring* point to the fact that our capability to forecast these calamities has not improved, in fact, despite more access to data and information than ever, we are not better equipped to understand the inner workings of societal downfalls. Have we been looking in the wrong directions, such as economic, social, and political determinants, and overseen the obvious, namely a changing psychological sentiment? Then it might be that all the information we are gathering and analyzing is just obscuring the actual trigger.

The structural factors often blamed for political violence and the collapse of nations, such as economic inequalities, ethnic or religious divides, perceived injustices of various types, do form the basis for grievances, but not necessarily for acting out on them. And these conditions might have persisted for generations, with most segments of the population always able to find a reason for feeling oppressed, even about events that no longer affect them or never even had, hence it appears that something to light the proverbial fuse is needed.

It is here that Freud's theories of a death drive fit in as a catalyst to change, a distinct psychological adjustment in the collective mindset. It does appear that once the death drive has sprung into motion, preventing it from erupting into a destructive mode, whether directed inwards with increasing number of suicides, drug abuse, and mental health issues, and/or outwardly manifested in political or religious violence, has proven difficult by historical accounts. Only a political leadership that is psychologically, rather than politically, astute can revert a death drive from materializing, either by directing it toward a group of scapegoats, typically political enemies, or providing outlets that are culturally acceptable and controllable which will allow them to retain, at least to some degree, the status quo, the *bread and circuses* approach providing an example that has survived throughout history. However, such strategies, for various reasons, rarely see their conclusions and often further repression is the prescribed remedy, resulting in accumulating pent-up aggressiveness that once released much like a spring coil erupts into corresponding levels of destruction and misery.

Whilst the immediate effects of the death drive can be terrifying, Freud posited that the ulterior objective carries altruistic properties as it seeks to rectify psychologically imbalances that threaten the mental well-being of mankind itself, thus the short-term side effects might be a necessary evil to ensure that mankind survives and can again prosper.

To Freud, a repressive psychological lifestyle is part and parcel of what being a well-adjusted citizen is about, being the flip side of civilization, but once these restraining attributes goes into overdrive, it awakens an urge to destroy that civilization. On the other hand, allowing for human instincts to freely express itself without constraints will inevitably lead to anarchy and chaos. Thus, it is about finding a delicate and dynamic middle road but with noted consequences, if deviating on either side, that take its toll on the human psyche. Insights on any relapses from a psychological equilibrium can be observed from statistics on the trending of the various forms of mental illnesses on one side, and the increasing levels of crime and violence in a nation marked by lawlessness on the other.

The activation of the death drive as a reaction to collective mental stagnation and as a spark to societal upheavals provides interesting explanatory powers, however, has been noticeably little researched. But a society that has become psychologically repressed and where natural outlets for human drives are denied, leaves clear marks that can be studied and applied as pre-cursors to forecast and time turmoil and uprisings. These pre-cursors can be found in demographics, such as increased suicide rates, increased use of alcohol and narcotics, lower life expectancy, and increased instances of mental illnesses. However, as most of these statistics are marred with measurement problems, issues

such as suicide, mental health issues and substance abuse in most countries carries great stigma, and thus tend to be underreported, for instance many traffic accidents, especially single car crashes, are often
thinly veiled suicides but rarely reported as such. It also comes down to
fluid definitions, in particular for mental illnesses where over time what
is considered to fall under its definition can vary, and significantly so,
as it also to some extent is dependent on the government's health budg-
ets and approach to mental health care. Hence, these metrics must be
studied together to rough out the edges and get a benchmark take on
when the status of the collective mind can be considered to develop in
an adverse direction. But, of course, such negative developments can
occur without a death drive activating, there are indeed other root
causes, increased numbers of suicide and alcoholism are observed in
economic recessions, however these increases tend to recede hastily as
economic conditions improve. To consider the death drive as the causal
factor, the increasing trends in deteriorating demographic metrics needs
to transcend the economic cycle, even contradict it. And the case studies
referred to, *World War I*, the *Fall of Communism in Eastern Europe* and the
Arab Spring, all provides little in terms of correlation between economic
depressions and societal breakdowns, the first case actually contradicting it. There are also additional manifestations to distinguish the ignition of the death drive, and that is in culture. The turn of the twentieth
century cultural critiques remarked on what they perceived as a growing trend of degeneration and decadence in art, where distortions of
what was deemed symmetrical aesthetics, through an accentuation of
the bizarre, the grotesque, and the monstrous which emerged as the prevailing art trends. In a culture that embraces the death drive there is a
noted decrease in artistic quality, and kitsch, such as pop art, social realism, comes to the forefront. In particular, themes around the morbid

can be noted, where horror stories and similar things become all the rage. Later research has also confirmed the link between a fascination for the morbid and psychological disturbances.

Obviously, in a pluralistic society multiple forces are at work simultaneously, and some of them will be contradictory, however if adverse demographic factors, and decadent and degenerate art forms are on the rise, these manifestations carry the hallmark of the death drive in force. What can then be expected?

As the psychological sentiments of the death drive seek to undermine the reigning doctrine, implicitly it will express itself politically, and this is where populist or revolutionary movements extend the (creative) destruction, sometimes emanating from the inner circles of power and then posing as reformists; in other instances, it will start as grass roots movements operated by leaders with charismatic qualities. From there on, efforts to prevent the death drive from holding sway over the population are usually futile.

This brings us to the key question, is the death drive at work in our current era? With Brexit in mind and the uncertainty over the future of the European Union, can by applying the death drive methodology help us understand whether it is facing its demise in the near future?

The suicidal tendencies of the West have been duly noted by some principal political commentators, including the conservative American analyst Jonah Goldberg in his *Suicide of the West: How the Rebirth of Tribalism, Populism, Nationalism, and Identity Politics is Destroying American Democracy* published in 2018. Albeit the title is alluding to a downfall of American democracy, its analysis extends to include a critique of Western culture itself. Much comes down to the reigning identity politics that implicitly segregate various groups in society, notably by ethnic and gender lines, with the risk of political violence in the cards by promoting some groups and demoting others through legislation and diversity quotas.

Concurring with Goldberg's thesis of Western culture at risk is Douglas Murray's best-seller *The Strange Death of Europe: Immigration, Identity, Islam* from 2017, taking aim at Muslim immigration to Europe and how over only a couple of decades they have come to constitute sizable minorities in most Western European countries. In addition to changing demographics, Murray argues that an ongoing spiritual de-generation undermines its future viability, where large chunks of the population have lost their devotion for the previous generation's stead-fast Christian beliefs, and which is exacerbated through mainstream politicians' attempts to replace it with a dogmatic worship of liberal globalism and multiculturalism, embracing these ideas to the extent that any critical remarks thereof have been the subject of harsh attacks, not seldom smeared as racism. However, such an ideology lacks both the psychological and intellectual depth when compared to *any* religion, and adherence to it has been shallow, with people, at best, regressing to parroting the empty slogans they are provided. And through the edu-cational system, and much of the traditional media and political parties, pro-actively downplaying historical Western contributions to art and science, extending to criticism and even to attempts to outright eradicate their mentioning altogether from education, have left many feeling robbed of their cultural inheritance.

Unfortunately, similarities with the repressive atmosphere of the Victorian era can be observed in the much of the Western world of today, curtailing independent thinking. In some universities and work-places, terms such as *trigger warnings* and *micro-aggressions* have been introduced to fend off any perceived unpleasant realities that confront neurotic illusions. To ensure emotional well-being and the *right* not to be offended, some university students demand to be protected from words, stories, ideas, and even everyday behavior deemed unpleasant, with the list constantly expanding. Words and phrases that at face value appear mundane can be viewed as malicious in the wrong context, be-ing micro-aggressions. To forewarn of any educational materials that can be considered confrontational or displeasing trigger warnings are issued to sensitive students. Even logic inference itself is under attack with demands to replace it with *emotional reasoning* that defines the cor-rectness of an argument on whether it causes negative emotions, such as if an opinion is considered offensive hence it must by default be er-roneous, regardless of whether it has been arrived at in a correct deduc-tive manner or not, with any further analysis being superfluous. The value and perceived objectivity of the interpretation of what constitutes an offensive remark rests with the party that manages to subscribe to the greatest level of *victimization*, typically linked to one's alignment to a certain group identity, as such the most victimized individual is likely to win the debate as any argument that falls out of their favor can be labelled as offensive and emotionally hurtful. By pulling the *I'm offended* card, any debate is thus concluded and won. Over time, of course, the bar for what can be publicly uttered is lowered to the point that open debates in effect become meaningless, as emotional conclusions reign over logic arguments. In such psychological surroundings evolved through reducing the outlets for free thinking, the risk of mental stag-nation is on the rise and it provides fertile ground for the death drive to activate.

What picture do some of the metrics of psychological health in the EU paint? As depicted in figure 1) the suicide rates and self-inflicted injuries for the EU and some of its key member states mostly have been coming down or staying relatively flat since the millennia shift up to 2015. And as highlighted in figure 2) whilst the life expectancy increased steadily for the first decade after 2000, for the last few years up to 2017, it has now flattened out, even started to decrease for the EU as a whole, including some of its key countries. With regards to alcohol and substance abuse, figures 3), 4) and 5) send a conflicting message, whilst alcohol related deaths have been falling from the millennia shift onwards, the last couple of years have seen a reversal of the trend and the numbers are now on the increase, albeit not distinctly. First admissions to drug treatment centers in the EU, however, have increased almost 30 percent from 2000 to 2014, and notably in France, Germany, and United Kingdom drug related deaths have increased significantly. And figure 6) highlights a significant increase in mental disorders in the EU and most of its key member states, with the number accelerating in the last few years, but not yet translating into an increase in the number of suicides.

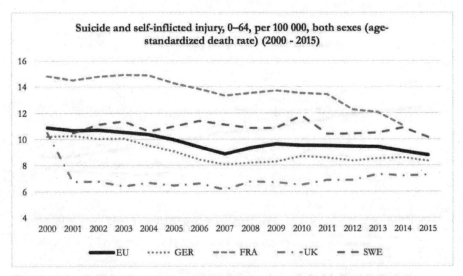

Figure 1) Suicide and self-inflicted injury, 0–64, per 100 000, both sexes (age-standardized death rate) 2000 - 2015. EU, Germany, France, United Kingdom & Sweden. Source: WHO European Health for All database (HFA-DB) https://gateway.euro.who.int/en/datasets/european-health-for-all-database/

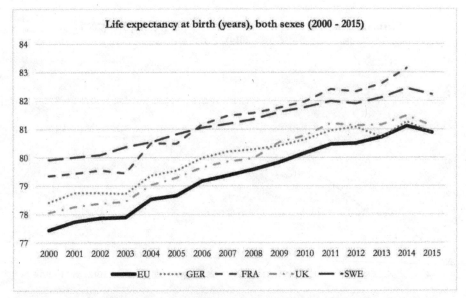

Figure 2) Life expectancy at birth, years (both sexes) 2000 - 2015. EU, Germany, France, United Kingdom & Sweden. Source: WHO European Health for All database (HFA-DB) https://gateway.euro.who.int/en/datasets/european-health-for-all-database/

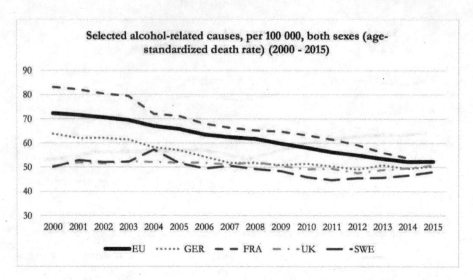

Figure 3) Selected alcohol-related causes, per 100 000, both sexes (age-standardized death rate) 2000 - 2015. EU, Germany, France, United Kingdom & Sweden. Source: WHO European Health for All database (HFA-DB) https://gateway.euro.who.int/en/datasets/european-health-for-all-database/

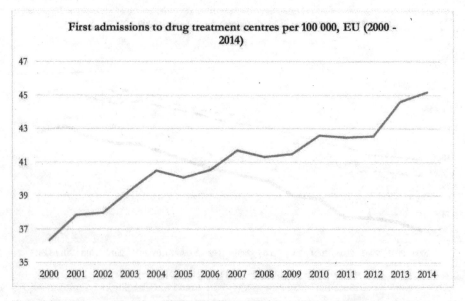

Figure 4) First admissions to drug treatment centres per 100 000, 2000 - 2014. European Union. Source: WHO European Health for All database (HFA-DB) https://gateway.euro.who.int/en/datasets/european-health-for-all-database/

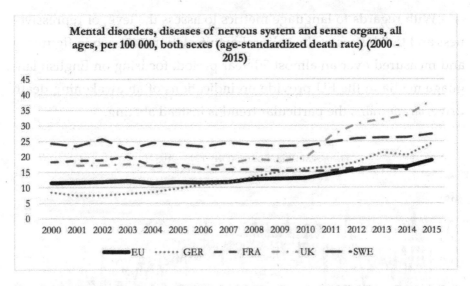

Figure 5) Mental disorders, diseases of nervous system and sense organs, all ages, per 100 000, both sexes (age-standardized death rate) 2000 - 2015. EU, Germany, France, United Kingdom & Sweden. Source: WHO European Health for All database (HFA-DB) https://gateway.euro.who.int/en/datasets/european-health-for-all-database/

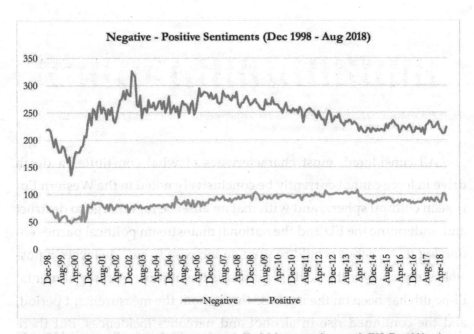

Figure 6) Measurements of negative and positive sentiments in English language media across the EU, Dec 1998 - Aug 2018. Source: Proprietary model

With regards to language metrics to assess the level of repressiveness and the themes of the cultural manifestations, as seen in figures 7)
and measured over an almost 20-year period, focusing on English language media in the EU provide no indications of an awakening death
drive, *au contraire*, the particular trend is instead abating.

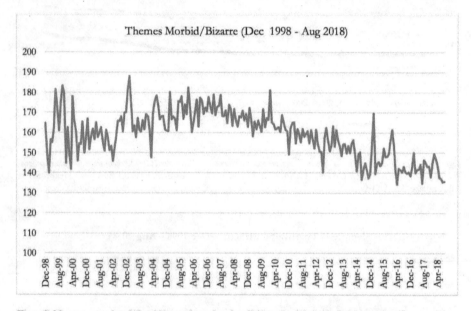

*Figure 7) Measurements of morbid and bizarre themes in culturally focused articles in English language media across the
EU, Dec 1998 - Aug 2018. Source:* Proprietary model

All considered, most characteristics of what constitutes a death
drive in force cannot currently be conclusively noted in the Western European cultural sphere, and with that an absence for an urge to destruct
and undermine the EU and the national mainstream political parties en-
dorsing it. A change would require an increase in suicide levels, a possible scenario over the next few years as the number of cases of mental
ill-health has been on the increase throughout the measurement period,
and the continued rise in alcohol and narcotics incidences. But there

would also have to be a change in the language that colors the percep-tions of the world with a more radicalized vocabulary and metaphorical reference that historically have preceded the outbreak of conflicts.

We are not there yet... and might never be.

But by applying the death drive methodology and understanding at what stages its various manifestations have advanced to, whether that be an increasingly dogmatic and repressive political atmosphere where 'unwelcomed' political views are silenced through various means, an art scene where the aesthetic quality is in decline replaced by the bizarre and morbid, and dramatically increased levels of psycholog-ical ill-health and suicides, the reader is thus equipped with a monitor to track for changes that can forebode, far ahead of others, the potential for an ominous future.

References

Chapter 1

"Free Will," in *The Stanford Encyclopedia of Philosophy*, edited by Edward N. Zalta, 2011.

Computational Neuroscience Research Group. Waterloo Centre for Theoretical Neuroscience. http://compneuro.uwaterloo.ca/ index.html (accessed January 1, 2019)

De Neys, Wim. "Dual processing in reasoning: Two systems but one reasoner." *Psychological Science* 17 (5), 2006.

Dijksterhuis, Ap, et al. "The Unconscious Mind" *Perspectives on Psychological Science*. January, 2008.

Dunne, Claire. *Carl Jung: Wounded Healer of the Soul: An Illustrated Biography*. London: Continuum International Publishing Group, 2002.

Ellenberger, Henri F. *The Discovery of the Unconscious: The History and Evolution of Dynamic Psychiatry*. New York: Basic Books, 1970.

Flora, Carlin. "*Gut Almighty*" Psychology Today 40(3), 2007.

Francis, Richard C. *Epigenetics: How Environment Shapes Our Genes*. New York: W. W. Norton & Company, 2012.

Freud, Anna. *The Ego and the Mechanisms of Defense*. London: Karnac Books, 1992.

Freud, Sigmund. *The Unconscious*. Penguin Modern Classics Translated Texts, 2005.

Freud, Sigmund. *Group Psychology and the Analysis of the Ego*. New York: Bantam Books, 1959.

Goodwyn, Erik D. *The Neurobiology of the Gods: How Brain Physiology Shapes the Recurrent Imagery of Myth and Dreams*. New York: Routledge, 2012.

Graziano, Michael S. A. *Consciousness and the Social Brain*. New York: Oxford University Press, 2013.

Human Brain Project. https://www.humanbrainproject.eu/ (accessed January 1, 2019)

Jung, CG. *The archetypes and the collective unconscious*. In Part 1: The Collected Works of C. G. Jung, translated by RFC Hull. Princeton, NJ: Princeton University Press, 1981. Vol. 9, 2nd edition.

Jung, CG. *Concerning the archetypes and the anima concept*. Part 1: The Collected Works of C. G. Jung, translated by RFC Hull. Princeton, NJ: Princeton University Press, 1981. Vol. 9, 2nd edition.

Kriegel, Uriah. *Current Controversies in Philosophy of Mind*. New York, NY: Taylor & Francis, 2014.

Mandal, Fatik Baran. *Textbook of Animal Behaviour*. Delhi: PHI Learning, 2010.

Maslow, Abraham H. "Instinct Theory Reexamined." In *Motivation and Personality*. New York: Harper & Row, 1954.

Merck Manual of Diagnosis and Therapy Home Edition - "Physical Examination." 06-077c. www.merckmanuals.com

Merriam-Webster Dictionary. "Unconscious." www.merriam-webster.com/dictionary/unconscious

Schwartz, Casey. "Tell it about your mother - Can brainscanning help save Freudian psychoanalysis?" *New York Times*, June 28, 2015. http://www.nytimes.com/2015/06/28/magazine/tell-it-aboutyour-mother.html (accessed January 1, 2019)

Sheehy, Noel & Forsythe, Alexandra. "Sigmund Freud." *Fifty Key Thinkers in Psychology*. London: Routledge, 2013.

Stein, Dan J. *Cognitive Science and the Unconscious*. Arlington, VA: American Psychiatric Publishing, 1997.

Sternberg, Robert J & Leighton, Jacqueline P. *The Nature of Reasoning*. Cambridge, MA: Cambridge University Press, 2004.

Stevens, Anthony & Rosen, David H. *The Two Million-Year-Old Self* (Carolyn and Ernest Fay Series in Analytical Psychology). College Station, TX: Texas A&M University Press, 2005.

The American Heritage Dictionary of the English Language. http:// ahdictionary.com/ (accessed January 1, 2019)

The Brain Initiative. https://braininitiative.nih.gov/index.htm (accessed January 1, 2019)

Wilson, Edward O. *Sociobiology: The New Synthesis*. Cambridge, MA: Belknap Press of Harvard University Press, 2000. 25th Anniversary edition.

Chapter 2

Bjerre, Poul Carl. *Death and Renewal*. New York: MacMillan, 1930.

Buss, David M. *Evolutionary psychology: the new science of the mind*. New York: Psychology Press, 2014.

Freud, Anna. *The Ego and the Mechanisms of Defense*. London, United Kingdom; Karnac Books, 1992.

Freud, Sigmund. *Beyond the Pleasure Principle* Translated by C.J.M. Hubback. London, 1922. Vienna: Intl. Psycho-analytical. New York: Bartleby.com, 2010. http://www.bartleby.com/276/ (accessed January 1, 2019)

Freud, Sigmund. *Civilization and Its Discontents*. London: Penguin, 2002.

Fromm, Erich. *The Sane Society* 2nd ed. New York: Routledge, 2014.

Ginot, Efrat. *The Neuropsychology of the Unconscious: Integrating Brain and Mind in Psychotherapy*. (Norton Series on Interpersonal Neurobiology). 1st ed. New York: W. W. Norton & Company, 2015.

Goel, V., Bruchel, C., Frith, C., Dolan, R. *Dissociation of mechanisms underlying syllogistic reasoning* NeuroImage. 12 (5), 2000. https://www.ncbi.nlm.nih.gov/pubmed/11034858 (accessed January 1, 2019)

Goel, V., Dolan, R. *Explaining modulation of reasoning by belief* Cognition 87 (1), 2003. http://www.sciencedirect.com/science/article/pii/ S00100 27702001853?via%3Dihub (accessed January 1, 2019)

Garssen, B. *Repression: Finding our way in the maze of concepts*. Journal of Behavioral Medicine 30 (6), December 2007. http://www.ncbi.nlm.nih.gov/pmc/articles/PMC2080858/pdf/ 10865_2007_ Article_9122. pdf (accessed January 1, 2019).

Hook, Derek. "Of Symbolic Mortification and 'Undead Life': Slavoj Žižek on the Death Drive." *Psychoanalysis and History*, Volume 18, Issue 2, 2016. http://www.euppublishing.com/doi/abs/10.3366/pah.2016. 0190? journalCode=pah (accessed January 1, 2019)

Igra, Ludvig. *På liv och död: Om destruktivitet och livsvilja*. Lund, Sweden: Studentlitteratur AB. 2003.

Johnston, Mark. *Self-Deception and the Nature of Mind Philosophy of Psychology: Debates on Psychological Explanation* Philosophy of Psychology (Debates on Psychological Explanation). Cambridge, United Kingdom: Blackwell Publishing, 1995.

Jung, C.G. *Two Essays on Analytical Psychology* translated by R.F.C. Hull, 2nd ed. Princeton, New Jersey: Princeton University Press, 1977.

Jung, C.G. *The Archetypes and the Collective Unconscious* translated by R.F.C. Hull, 2nd ed. Princeton, New Jersey: Princeton University Press, 1981.

Kaba, Fatos, et al. "Solitary Confinement and Risk of Self-Harm Among Jail Inmates." *American Journal of Public Health*, 104 (3), March 2014. http://ajph.aphapublications.org/doi/pdf/10.2105/AJPH.2013.301 742 (accessed January 1, 2019)

Marcuse, Herbert. *Eros and Civilization: A Philosophical Inquiry into Freud.* New ed. Boston, MA: Beacon Press, 1974.

McDougall, William. *An Introduction to Social Psychology*, 2nd ed. London, United Kingdom: Methuen & Co., 1909.

McLaughlin, Brian P., Oksenberg Rorty, Amélie. *Perspectives on Self-Deception (Topics in Philosophy)*. Berkeley and Los Angeles, California: University of California Press, 1988.

Meltzer, Howard; et al. *Non-Fatal Suicidal Behaviour Among Adults aged 16 to 74, Great Britain.* London, United Kingdom: National Statistics, The Stationery office, 2000. http://webarchive.nationalarchives.gov.uk/20160128193136/http://www.ons.gov.uk/ons/rel/psychiatric-morbidity/non-fatal-suicidal-behaviour-among-adults/aged-16-74-in-great-britain/index.html (accessed January 1, 2019)

Näslund, Görel Kristina. *Borderline personlighetsstörning: Uppkomst, symptom, behandling, prognos.* Stockholm, Sweden: Natur och kultur, 1998.

Rea, K., Aiken, F., Borastero, C. *Building Therapeutic Staff: Client Relationships with Women Who Self-Harm. Women's Health Issues*, 7 (2), 1997. http://www.whijournal.com/article/S1049-3867(96)00112-0/pdf (accessed January 1, 2019)

Roazen, Paul. *Freud and His Followers.* New York: Alfred A. Knopf, 1975.

Schwartz, C. "Tell it about your mother – Can brainscanning help save Freudian psychoanalysis." *New York Times*. June 24, 2015. http://www.nytimes.com/2015/06/28/magazine/tellit-about-your-mother.html?_r=0 (accessed January 1, 2019).

Segal, Hanna. *Introduction to the Work of Melanie Klein*. London, United Kingdom: Karnac Books, 1988.

Solms, Mark. *The Neuropsychology of Dreams: A Clinico-anatomical Study*. (Institute for Research in Behavioral Neuroscience Series), 1st ed. New York: Psychology Press, 2015.

Chapter 3

Bartholomew, Robert E.; Goode, Erich. *Mass Delusions and Hysterias: Highlights from the Past Millennium*. Committee for Skeptical Inquiry May-June 2000. 24http://www.csicop.org/si/show/mass_delusions_and_hysterias_highlights_from_the_past_millennium (accessed January 1, 2019).

Bicchieri, C. *The Grammar of Society: The Nature and Dynamics of Social Norms*. New York: Cambridge University Press, 2006.

Bostock, William. "Collective and Individual Depression: Is there a causal link?" *Perspectives*, 2001, 1 January.

Cialdini, RB; Goldstein, NJ. *Social influence: Compliance and conformity*. Annual Review of Psychology, 55, 2004. http://www2.psych.ubc.ca/~schaller/Psyc591Readings/ Cialdini Goldstein2004.pdf (accessed January 1, 2019)

Cohen, Stanley. *Folk Devils and Moral Panics: Creation of Mods and Rockers*. St. Albans: Paladin, 1973.

Diagnostic and Statistical Manual of Mental Disorders, 4th Edition. 2000.

Durkheim, E. *The Rules of Sociological Method and Selected Texts on Sociology and its Method*. New York: Free Press, 2013.

Encyclopædia Britannica Online. "Taboo." Encyclopædia Britannica Inc., 2012. http://global.britannica.com/topic/taboo-sociology (accessed January 1, 2019).

Freud, Sigmund. *Beyond the Pleasure Principle, Group Psychology and Other Works*. In Standard Edition, XVIII (1920-1922). London: Hogarth, 1955.

Freud, Sigmund. *Civilization and Its Discontents*. In *Civilization, Society and Religion*. London: W W Norton & Co, Inc., 1987.

Freud, Sigmund. *Group Psychology and the Analysis of the Ego*. London, Vienna: The International Psychoanalytical Press, 1922.

Freud, Sigmund. *Moses and Monotheism*. 1939. New York: Martino Fine Books, 2010 reprint.

Freud, Sigmund. *Totem and Taboo, Some Points of Agreement between the mental Lives of Savages and Neurotics*. London: Routledge & Kegan Paul, 1950.

Gay, Peter. *Freud: A Life for Our Time*. London: W W Norton & Co Inc., 1989.

Gurr, Ted R. *Why men rebel*. Princeton, NJ: Princeton University Press, 1970.

Hatfield, E.; Cacioppo, J. T.; Rapson, R. L. *Emotional Contagion*. Current Directions in Psychological Science 2, 1993.

Hinsie, L.E.; Campbell, R.J. *Psychiatric dictionary*. 4th edition. London: Oxford University Press, 1973.

Hopper, Earl. *The social unconscious: Theoretical considerations*. Group Analysis. Special Issue 34, 2001.

Janis, I.L. *Groupthink: Psychological Studies of Policy Decisions and Fiascoes*. 2nd edition. Boston, MA: Cengage Learning, 1982.

Jones, Ernest. *The Life and Work of Sigmund Freud*. London: Pelican Books, 1964.

Jones, Marsha; Jones, Emma. *Mass Media (Skills-Based Sociology)*. London: Palgrave Macmillan, 1999.

Jones, Timothy. *Mass Psychogenic Illness: Role of the Individual Physician.* American Family Physician 62, 2000.

Jung, C. G. *Collected Works of C.G. Jung, Volume 7: Two Essays in Analytical Psychology.* New Jersey: Princeton University Press, 1967.

Jung, C. G. *On the Nature of the Psyche.* Vol. 8 of *The Collected Works of C. G. Jung,* trans. R. F. C. Hull, 2nd ed. Princeton, NJ: Princeton University Press, 1981.

Lake, David A.; Rothchild, Donald. "The Origins and Management of Ethnic Conflict." *International Security,* Vol. 21, No. 2, Autumn 1996.

Magee, G.A. *Zeitgeist, The Hegel Dictionary.* London, United Kingdom: Continuum International Publishing Group, 2011.

Mass, Weir E. *Mass Sociogenic Illness.* Canadian Medical Association Journal 172, 2005.

Odajnyk Walter V. *Jung and Politics: The Political and Social Ideas of C. G. Jung.* Lincoln, NE: Authors Choice Press, 2007.

Schoenewolf, G. "Emotional Contagion: Behavioral Induction in Individuals and Groups." *Modern Psychoanalysis* 15, 1990.

Shaffer, L.S. "Durkheim's aphorism, the justification hypothesis, and the nature of social facts." *Sociological Viewpoints.* Fall Issue 2006. https://www.questia.com/library/journal/1P3-1639680671/durkheim-s-aphorism-the-justification-hypothesis (accessed January 1, 2019)

Tetlock, PE; Orie, KV; Elson, B; Green, MC; Lerner, JS. "The psychology of the unthinkable: Taboo trade-offs, forbidden base rates, and heretical counterfactuals." *Journal of Personality and Social Psychology,* 2000. http://www.ncbi.nlm. nih.gov/pubmed/10821194 (accessed January 1, 2019)

Turner, ME; Pratkanis, AR. "Twenty-five years of groupthink theory and research: Lessons from the evaluation of a theory." *Organizational Behavior and Human Decision Processes* 73, 1998. http://www.soc. ucsb.edu/faculty/friedkin/Syllabi/ Soc147/Week5Req1Reading.pdf (accessed January 1, 2019)

Updegraff, J.A., Silver R.C., Holman E.A. "Searching for and finding meaning in collective trauma: results from a national longitudinal study of the 9/11 terrorist attacks." *J Pers Soc Psychol.* Sep 2008.

von Franz, M.-L. *Archetypal Dimensions of the Psyche.* Boston, MA: Shambala Publications Inc., 1999.

Weinberg, Haim. "So What is this Social Unconscious Anyway?" *Group Analysis.* Volume 40, Issue 3, 2007.

Wesley, S.P., Nola, J.M., Cialdini, R.B., Goldstein, N.J. Griskevicius, V., "The constructive, destructive, and reconstructive power of social norms." *Psychological Science* 18 (5), May 2007, pp. 429-434. http://assets.csom.umn.edu/assets/118375.pdf (accessed January 1, 2019).

Chapter 4

Aristotle. *Politics.* Indianapolis: Hackett Publishing Company, 1998.

Cucuta, Radu-Alexandru. "*Theories of Revolution: The Generational Deadlock*" Challenges of the Knowledge Society, CKS, Bucuresti: Pro Universitaria, 2013.

Brinton, Crane. *The Anatomy of Revolution.* New York: Prentice-Hall, vintage edition, 1965.

Davies, James C. "Toward a Theory of Revolution" *American Sociological Review*, Vol. 27, No. 1., Feb 1962.

Glubb, John Bagot. *The Fate of Empires and Search for Survival.* Edinburgh, United Kingdom: Blackwood, 1978.

Goldstone, Jack A. "Toward a Fourth Generation of Revolutionary Theory" *Annual Review of Political Science*, Vol. 4. 2001.

Goldstone, Jack A. "Rethinking Revolutions: Integrating Origins, Processes, and Outcomes" *Comparative Studies in South Asia, Africa, and the Middle East*, Vol. 29, No. 1., 2009.

Jung, C. G. *Civilization in Transition*, Vol. 10 of *The Collected Works of C. G. Jung*, trans. R. F. C. Hull, 2nd ed. Princeton, NJ: Princeton University Press, 1981.

Jung, C.G. *The Psychology of the Unconscious*, Vol. 7 of *The Collected Works of C. G. Jung*, trans. R. F. C. Hull, 2nd ed. London, UK: Routledge, 1990. 1917/1926/1943 reprint.

Jung, C.G. *The Undiscovered Self*. Vol. 10 of *The Collected Works of C. G. Jung*, trans. R. F. C. Hull, 2nd ed. London, UK: Routledge, 1991. 1957 reprint.

Keddie, Nikki R (ed) & Goldstone, Jack A. *Debating Revolutions, Predicting Revolutions: Why We Could (and Should) Have Foreseen the Revolutions of 1989–1991 in the U.S.S.R. and Easter Europe*. New York: NYU Press; 1st edition, 1995.

Lewin, Nicholas. *Jung on War, Politics and Nazi Germany: Exploring the Theory of Archetypes and the Collective Unconscious*. London, UK: Karnac Books, 1st edition, 2009.

Łobaczewski, Andrzej. *Political Ponerology: A Science on the Nature of Evil Adjusted for Political Purposes*. Grande Prairie: Red Pill Press, 2006.

Plato. *The Republic*. Indianapolis: Hackett Publishing Company; 2nd edition, 1992.

Skocpol, Theda. *States and Social Revolutions: A Comparative Analysis of France, Russia and China*. Cambridge, UK: Cambridge University Press, 1979.

Tocqueville, Alexis de. *The Old Regime and the French Revolution*. Mineola, NY: Dover Publication, 2010.

von Franz, M-L. *Psyche and matter.* New York: Random House Incorporated, 1992.

Chapter 5

Arns, Inke; Sasse, Sylvia. "Subversive Affirmation. On Mimesis as Strategy of Resistance." Editorial, *Maska*, Ljubljana. Spring 2006 issue.

Bailey, Hamilton. *Demonstrations of physical signs in clinical surgery.* (1st ed.). Bristol: J. Wright and Sons, 1927.

Björtorp, P., Holm, G., & Rosmond, R. *Neuroendokrina störningar ger stressrelaterad sjukdom. "Civilisationssyndromet" ett växande hälsoproblem.* Läkartidningen, 99. 1999.

Boeree, C. George. *A Bio-Social Theory of Neurosis.* 2002. http://webspace.ship.edu/ cgboer/genpsyneurosis.html

Calhoun, John B. "The Social Aspects of Population Dynamics." *Journal of Mammalogy.* American Society of Mammalogists. 33 (2), 1952.

Durkheim, Emile. *The Division of Labour in Society.* New York: Free Press, 1997. Translated.

Freud, Sigmund. *Formulations on the Two Principles of Mental Functioning.* London: Routledge, 1 edition, 1911. 2016 reprint.

Freud, Sigmund. *Group Psychology and the Analysis of the Ego.* New York: W.W. Norton & Company, Revised edition, 1921. 1990 reprint.

Freud, Sigmund. *"Totem and Taboo: Resemblances Between the Mental Lives of Savages and Neurotics".* New York: W. W. Norton & Company; The Standard Edition, 1913. 1990 Translated.

Heffernan, Michael. "The Politics of the Map in the Early Twentieth Century." *Cartography and Geographic Information Science,* 29/3, 2002.

Horney, Karen. *Neurosis and Human Growth: The Struggle Toward Self-Realization.* W.W. Norton & Company, Inc., 1950.

Jaspers, Karl. *General Psychopathology - Volumes 1 & 2.* translated by J. Hoenig and Marian W. Hamilton. Baltimore and London: Johns Hopkins University Press, 1997.

Johannisson, Karin. *Den mörka kontinenten: kvinnan, medicinen och fin-de-siècle.* Stockholm, Sweden: Nordstedts Förlag, 1994.

Johannisson, Karin. "Om begreppet kultursjukdom." *Läkartidningen* nr 44, volym 105, 2008.

Johannisson, Karin. "Trötthetens problem har gamla anor." *Svenska Dagbladet.* 29 November 2002.

Jung, C.G. *Collected Works of C.G. Jung,* Volume 7: *Two Essays in Analytical Psychology.* New Jersey: Princeton University Press, 1967.

Jung, C. G. *Collected Works of C.G. Jung,* Volume 10: *Civilization and Transition, Wotan.* London: Routledge and Kegan Paul, 1970.

Maxwell, Catherine. "Theodore Watts-Dunton's 'Aylwin (1898)' and the Reduplications of Romanticism." *The Yearbook of English Studies* 37.1 (2007).

Nordau, Max. *Degeneration.* Nebraska: University of Nebraska Press; Reprinted edition, 1892. Translated 1993.

Pick, Daniel. *Faces of Degeneration. A European disorder, c.1848-c.1918.* Cambridge, UK: Cambridge University Press, 1989.

Szakolczai, Arpad. "Liminality and Experience: Structuring transitory situations and transformative events" *International Political Anthropology,* 2 (1), 2009.

The ICD-10 Classification of Mental and Behavioural Disorders, Clinical descriptions and diagnostic guidelines http://www.who.int/classifications/icd/en/bluebook.pdf

Thomassen, B. "The Uses and Meanings of Liminality." *International Political Anthropology,* 2 (1), 2009.

Trostle, James A. *Epidemiology and Culture*. Cambridge Studies in Medical Anthropology. Cambridge: Cambridge University Press, 2005.

Unwin, Joseph Daniel. "Monogamy as a Condition of Social Energy." *The Hibbert Journal*, Vol. XXV, 1927.

Unwin, Joseph Daniel. *Sex and Culture*. London: Oxford University Press, 1934.

Weber, Max. *Essays in Economic Sociology*. Princeton: Princeton University Press; First edition, translated, 1999.

Yamada N., Nakajima S., Noguchi T. "Age at onset of delusional disorder is dependent on the delusional theme." *Acta Psychiatrica Scandinavica*. 97 (2), February 1988.

Zeev, Sternhell. "Crisis of Fin-de-siècle Thought." *International Fascism: Theories, Causes and the New Consensus*. London and New York, 1998.

Chapter 6

Aras, Bülent; Falk, Richard. "Five years after the Arab Spring: a critical evaluation." *Third World Quarterly*. 37 (12), 2016.

Alfadhel, Khalifa. *The Failure of the Arab Spring*. Cambridge, United Kingdom: Cambridge Scholars Publishing, 2016.

Aron, Leon. "Everything You Think You Know About the Collapse of the Soviet Union Is Wrong." *Foreign Policy*. 20 June 2011. https://foreign-policy.com/2011/06/20/everything-you-think-you-know-about-the-collapse-of-the-soviet-union-is-wrong/ (accessed January 1 2019)

Baudelot, Christian; Establet, Roger. *Suicide: The Hidden Side of Modernity*. Cambridge, United Kingdom; Polity Press, 2008.

Brownlee, Jason; Masoud, Tarek; Reynold, Andrew. *The Arab Spring: the politics of transformation in North Africa and the Middle East*. Oxford, United Kingdom: Oxford University Press, 2013.

Eksteins, Modris. *Rites of Spring*. Boston: First Mariner Books, 2000.

Freud. Sigmund; Einstein, Albert. *Why War? A Correspondence Between Albert Einstein and Sigmund Freud*. Published by the Peace Pledge Union with the permission of the International Institute of Intellectual Co-operation of the League of Nations, 1939.

Friedman, Thomas. "The Other Arab Spring." *The New York Times*, 7 April 2012.

Griffin, Roger. *The Meaning of 'Sacrifice' in the First World War*. Paper adapted from: Griffin, R., Modernism and Fascism. New York: Palgrave Macmillan, 2007. https://www.libraryofsocialscience.com/essays/griffin-the-meaning/index.html (accessed January 1 2019)

Haslam, N. "Dehumanization: An Integrated Review." *Personality and Social Psychology Review*, 10, 2006.

Havel, Vaclav. *En dåre i Prag: brev, tal, texter 1975-1990*. Stockholm, Sweden; Symposion, transl. Karin Mossdal, 1990.

Heleniak, Tim; Motivans, Albert. "A Note on Glasnost' and the Soviet Statistical System." *Soviet Studies*, Vol. 43, No. 3, 1991.

Lifton, Robert Jay. "Beyond psychic numbing: a call to awareness." *American Journal of Orthopsychiatry*, 52 (4), October, 1982.

Maddison, Angus. *The World Economy. Volume 2: Historical Statistics*. Paris, France: Development Centre Studies – OECD, 2006.

Malia, Martin. *Russia under Western Eyes: From the Bronze Horseman to the Lenin Mausoleum*. Cambridge; Belknap Press of Harvard University Press, 2000.

McCauley, Clark; Moskalenko, Sophia. *Friction: How Radicalization Happens to Them and Us*. New York: Oxford University Press, 2011.

Mokdad, Ali H.: et al. "The burden of mental disorders in the Eastern Mediterranean region, 1990–2015: findings from the global burden of disease 2015 study." *Int J Public Health* 63 (Suppl 1), 2018.

Mondofacto.com, "Scapegoating," www.mondofacto.com/ (accessed January 1 2019)

Nylund, Karl-Erik. *Att leka med elden: Sekternas värld.* Sverige: Selling & Partner, 2., omarb. uppl., 2004.

Pape, Robert. *Dying to Win: The Strategic Logic of Suicide Terrorism.* New York: Random House, 2005.

Perrin, Noel; Godine, David R. *Dr. Bowdler's Legacy: a history of expurgated books in England and America.* Boston: Nonpare, 2nd ed orig 1969, 1992.

Sullivan, Charles J. "Riding the Revolutionary Wave: America, The Arab Spring and the Autumn of 1989." *The Washington Review of Turkish and Eurasian Affairs.* Rethink Institute, April, 2011.

Todd, Emmanuel. *The Final Fall: An Essay on the Decomposition of the Soviet Sphere.* New York: Karz Publishers, transl. orig. 1976, 1979.

Toynbee, Arnold J. *A Study of History,* Vol. 1: Abridgement of Volumes I-VI and Vol. 2: Abridgement of Volumes VII-X. New York: Oxford University Press; Revised ed. Edition, 1987.

Wilner and Dubouloz. "Homegrown terrorism and transformative learning: an interdisciplinary approach to understanding radicalization." *Global Change, Peace, and Security,* 22:1, 2010.

Wood, Vincent. "British Muslim leader says May MUST crack down on prison radicalisation to beat terror." *Sunday Express,* March 25, 2017.

Wright, Alexa. *Monstrosity: The Human Monster in Visual Culture.* London, United Kingdom: I.B. Tauris & Co. Ltd., 2013.

Chapter 7

deMause, Lloyd. *The New psychohistory.* New York, NY: Psychohistory Press, 1975.

Jackendoff, R. *The architecture of the language faculty*. Cambridge, MA: MIT Press, 1997.

Keen, Sam. *Faces of the Enemy: Reflections of the Hostile Imagination*. New York, NY: Harper & Row, Publishers; 1st edition, 1991.

Kovecses, Zoltan. *Metaphor, A Practical Introduction*. New York, NY: Oxford University Press, 2nd edition, 2010.

Lakoff, George P. and Johnson, Mark L. *Metaphors We Live By*. Chicago, IL: University of Chicago, 2nd edition, 2003.

McCauley, C. and Moskalenko, S. "Mechanisms of political radicalization: Pathways toward terrorism." *Terrorism and Political Violence*, 20(3), 2008.

Morrison, Rodger. "New Method of Identifying Archetypal Symbols and their Associated Meanings." *European Journal of Social Sciences*. 27, 2011.

Pennebaker, J. W. and Chung, C. K. "Computerized text analysis of al-Qaeda transcripts." *The Content Analysis Reader*, K. Krippendorf and M. A. Bock (red), Sage. 2008.

Pennebaker, J. W. and Chung, C. K. *Language and social dynamics*. University of Texas at Austin, Technical Report 1318. 2012.

Pennebaker, J. W.; Francis, M. E. and Booth, R. J. *Linguistic inquiry and word count (liwc): A text analysis program*. New York, NY: Erlbaum Publishers, 2001.

Pennebaker, J.; Mehl, M. and Niederhoffer, K. "Psychological aspects of natural language use: Our words, our selves." *Annual Review of Psychology*, vol. 54, no. 1, 2003.

Smith, A.G. "From words to action: Exploring the relationship between a group's value references and its likelihood of engaging in terrorism." *Studies in Conflict and Terrorism*, 27(5), 2004.

Tausczik, Y. and P.J.W. "The psychological meaning of words: Liwc and computerized text analysis methods." *Journal of Language and Social Psychology*, vol. 29, no. 1, March 2010.

Victoroff, J. "The mind of the terrorist a review and critique of psychological approaches." *Journal of Conflict resolution*, 49(1), 2005.

ABOUT THE AUTHOR

Niklas Hageback has an extensive background in psychology working with behavioral finance; modelling irrational collective behavior at tier-one financial institutions and consulting firms, such as Deutsche Bank, KPMG, and Goldman Sachs, where he held regional executive management and project oversight roles in both Europe and Asia. More recently his focus is on cognitive psychology and he is managing a portfolio of software start-up firms that are developing Artificial Intelligence applications mimicking human behavior.

His previous bestselling books include *The Mystery of Market Movements: An Archetypal Approach to Investment Forecasting and Modelling* (2014), in which he proposes an alternative psychoanalytical methodology to forecasting trends and bubbles in financial markets. *The Virtual Mind: Designing the Logic to Approximate Human Thinking*, published in 2017, details in-depth and multidisciplinary research that outlines a blue-print which defines the underpinnings for creating machine generated human thinking through approximating the mind. *Idiots breed Id-*

iots: Why men no longer are created equal was released in 2018 and provides an up-to-date account of the changing demographics due to the ongoing automation of society and the cognitive demands of the knowledge-based economy. He has also published a number of research papers in the areas of finance and AI.

Mr. Hageback is an avid athlete, in particular long-distance running and powerlifting in which he holds the Asian Champion title.

INDEX